THE GAVIOTA LAND

Gaviota

The Gaviota Land

A Glimpse into California History from a Bend on El Camino Real

by
MERLYN CHESNUT

FITHIAN PRESS • SANTA BARBARA, 1993

*I would like to dedicate this book to all the many people who have known and
loved the land and to all those who would like to do so,
with special recognition to Charlie Foode, "Gaviota Charlie."*

Published by Fithian Press
Post Office Box 1525
Santa Barbara, CA 93102

Book design by Eric Larson

LIBRARY OF CONGRESS CATALOGING-IN-PUBLICATION DATA:
Chesnut, Merlyn
The Gaviota Land : a glimpse into California history from a bend on El Camino Real / Merlyn
    Chesnut.
p. cm.
Includes bibliographical references and index.
ISBN 1-56474-051-X
1. Gaviota Region (Calif.)—History. I. Title.
F869.G25C48 1993
979.4"91"00946—dc20   92-43995
    CIP

Thanks to the following for permission to reprint many of the illustrations contained in this book:

LeRoy Begg, 82
Jim Blakley, 85
Steve Bond, 199
California State Archives, 44
California State Mining Bureau, 163
Caltrans, 111, 113
Bob Carpenter, 162
Harry Day, 151, 153, 156
Howard Deets, 18, 118
Rose Dutra, 184
Jack Feliz, 131
Estelle Fraters, 162, 204
Inez and August George, 164
Mrs. W. Hall, 69
Walter Henning, 169, 211
John James Hollister III, 142
Jay Lambert, 62
Eric Larson, 31, 38, 66, 78, 92, 107, 157, 215, 223, 227
Cesarina Loustalot, 82, 112, 121, 122, 135, 136, 139, 143, 183
Lompoc Valley Historical Society, 39, 49, 59, 69, 80, 84, 87, 89, 94, 96, 99, 103, 106, 109, 128, 130, 132, 155, 163, 164, 220

Lompoc Murals Society and Robert Thomas, 27
Joe and Helen Luis, 165
John McDonell, 215
Ronald Nielsen, 127, 134, 168
Bob Parker, 189, 205
Dave Rutherford, 217
Santa Barbara Historical Society, 22, 35, 65, 73, 83, 100, 104, 106, 109, 110, 142, 144, 181, 162, 233
Santa Barbara Library, 165
Santa Barbara News-Press, 194, 198, 234
Santa Ynez Valley News, 58
Alora Spanne, 177
Hank Thygesen, 183
Dev Vrat, 233
Dutch Wilson, 150, 151
Paul Yrigollen and Lompoc Museum, 27

CONTENTS

LIST OF ILLUSTRATIONS

MAPS

ACKNOWLEDGEMENTS

There are many people who helped me gather this information. I am grateful for the assistance of the Lompoc *Record*, the Santa Barbara *News-Press*, the Santa Ynez Valley *News*, the Lompoc Murals Society, the Lompoc Museum, the Lompoc Valley Historical Society, the Santa Barbara Historical Society, and the Santa Ynez Historical Society.

I would like to express my appreciation to: Jinny Armas, Arnold Avila, Mary Balaam, LeRoy Begg, Jim Blakley, Steve Bond, Isaac Bonilla, Steven Briggs with Ogden Environmental, Steve Brown, Bob Burleson with Chevron U.S.A., Gertrude Burmester, Juanita Centeno, Tom Clancy, Grace Humphries Coleman, Frank Cordero, Grace Cota, Mel and Ruth Creps, Harry Crompe, Harry Day, Howard Deets, Rose Dutra, Donald Eittreim, Jack Feliz, Dennis Fitzgerald, Rena Fitzgerald, Peggy Fletcher, Charlie Foode, Estelle and Johnny Fraters, Inez & August George, Don Hansen, Caroline Henning, Walter Henning, John James Hollister III, Neal Kuzee, Jay Lambert, Dean and June Limes, Randy Lindros, Phyllis Lotz, Cesarina Loustalot, Jean Loustalot, Joe and Helen Luis, Worth Lundin, Mike Lunsford, Mike Madden with All American Pipeline, Myra Manfrina, Rose Marchbanks, Jane McNinamin, Russell Mickey, Stephen Moat, Ronald Nielsen, Tony Ochoa, Marilyn Oliver, Supervisor Dianne Owens, Greg Pensa, Robert Petersen, A. Dibblee Poett, Michael Redmon, Attilo Rivaldi, Jim Russell, Dave Rutherford, Bernard Saralegui, Alora and Walter Spanne, Gene Stevens, Dale Stone, Luzina Tautrim, Robert Thomas, Hank Thygesen, Donna Tucker, Dev Vrat, Dutch Wilson, Myrna Wise, and Paul Yrigollen.

Many took the time to tell me their stories and share part of their past in relation to the Gaviota Land; others provided pictures, maps, and other information. Special appreciation is extended to Bob Carpenter for postal information. I am especially grateful for my husband's assistance, patience, and understanding in this endeavor.

THE GAVIOTA LAND

The Gaviota Land.

Introduction

Many small areas of California often go unmentioned in larger works on the history of the state, yet many of these places have played large roles in the development of the California we know today. Each locale has its own unique story with its own characters and its own events, and some of these have been more influential than mere acreage would imply.

So it is with the Gaviota Land, a small section of coastal California along El Camino Real (the King's Highway—the original road connecting the chain of Spanish missions), lying east of Point Conception. It includes the historic Gaviota Pass, Gaviota Beach, and the surrounding areas. Although Gaviota is a small area, it has long been prominent in California history.

Whereas most of the California coast runs north and south, at Point Conception the land makes a dramatic ninety-degree turn and runs almost due east to Ventura, forming a rare south-facing coastline. This unusual configuration has contributed many unique aspects to the Gaviota Land. For example, during the winter months, the sun both rises and sets over the ocean. More importantly, this bend also creates the Santa Barbara Channel, bounded on the outside by the Channel Islands. Anacapa, Santa Cruz, Santa Rosa, and San Miguel are the closest to Gaviota and form a natural sea break that guards the coast from the powerful and relentless Pacific Ocean. The channel is an ocean corridor that has affected life for thousands of years, both on land and on the sea.

U.S. Highway 101, which passes through the Gaviota Land, is one of California's most important transportation arteries. From Ventura westward it parallels the ocean waves, but at Gaviota it turns abruptly to the north and crosses Gaviota Pass. The pass, a narrow slit among high, steep

El Camino Real turns eastward at Gaviota.

cliffs, is one of the oldest passes of historical significance in California and one of the few in the world that are so close to sea level. It is the western-most of the routes connecting southern and central California, and for many centuries it was the only gateway between the Pacific and the many rural communities that lie in the inland valleys of Santa Barbara County.

Thus the Gaviota area is often thought of as a "crossroads" of Califor-nia. Its mountainous terrain is considered a geological boundary between the northern and southern sections of the state, and it has long been the political partition between the northern and southern sections of Santa Barbara County. This, in turn, has often resulted in a division of local government into two disparate areas of political philosophy, for things of-ten look different on opposite sides of Gaviota Pass.

In this book an attempt has been made to collect as much information as possible about this fascinating region, although its history is so long and diverse that there are doubtless some inadvertent omissions. The general plan has been to present this information in chronological order as much as possible, although in some cases the subject matter has demanded a more thematic approach in order to preserve continuity.

As is true of any other place, Gaviota has experienced many changes and will never again be as it was in the past. Ages, eras, and mankind have made manifold alterations, but through the crevices of time, the past of this land and its people are still visible as shadows of the history of our state. Just as it is a gateway from the sea to the valleys, so Gaviota is a gateway into the yesterdays of California.

CHAPTER I
The Early Land and Its Inhabitants

The Gaviota Land was formed thousands of years ago when a series of enormous earthquakes fractured the Pacific coast and violent volcanic activity caused massive twisting and wrenching of the land, altering the structure of the earth. The nearby Channel Islands are thought to have been connected to the mainland before being severed from it, as the sea level in the channel rose and fell drastically with the changing earth. About 500,000 years ago, it is believed, the sea was almost 400 feet higher than it is now; it probably reached its present level around 6,000 years ago. During upheavals, the fissured rock structure of the Santa Ynez Range broke at Gaviota to form the pass, and the horizontal strata at the beach tilted to become almost vertical.

The Gaviota Land became covered with a forest of oaks and green grassland, with a profusion of beautiful wildflowers in spring. Tall grasses sheltered abundant wildlife years ago. Mountain lions and large bears roamed through the canyons, and herds of deer and many other animals grazed in the hills, including the mammoth with its hairy skin and ridged molar teeth. Thousands of otters, seals, and sea lions were on the shore, and numerous California condors, now almost extinct, were in the high mountains.

Gaviota Pass is a very constricted crevice in the towering limestone rock walls, and the creek at the base of these walls was a raging torrent from heavy rains. (Tree rings have been used to indicate what large amounts of rain once fell, and if information from them is accurate, a phenomenal 360 inches of rain came down in 1568.) Abundant moss, green ferns, and other native shrubs and plants adhered to the sides of the

Gaviota Pass, once a rocky wilderness.

pass, and large boulders often tumbled from its summit to the sea.

Three different groups of native inhabitants are believed to have lived at different times in the Gaviota coastal area, where both mountains and sea provided protection. The first known group was the Oak Grove People, who were there from 8,000-10,000 years ago. Their villages were close to thick oak groves and built on the crest of elevated ground to escape the great rains of torrential storms. Acorns were their staple food. Skills and implements for hunting and fishing are thought to have been limited, and pottery may not have been perfected. David Banks Rogers, an authority on the early Chumash, author, and first director of the Santa Barbara Museum of Natural History, believes the Oak Grove People lived high on the eastern promontory of Gaviota Creek.

The Hunting People followed. They were more nomadic, and it is believed that they had improved weapons. Knowledge of both of these early cultures is very limited, however, and the rains and winds of time have reclaimed most of the evidence of these early humans. They were supplanted, hundreds of years later, by the Chumash, who were on the Gaviota coast over 1,000 years ago.

The Chumash

These more advanced native people, with autonomous societies and distinct geographic territories, were in the Gaviota Land when the Spanish came, and the Spaniards' diaries contributed written information on their culture. "Chumash" refers to the entire cultural group, which extended along the California coast from Los Angeles County to San Luis Obispo County; "Canaliño" (channel dweller) refers to the coastal Chumash. There were eight regional linguistic dialects in local use; Purisimeño, Ineseño, Barbareño, and Cruzeño reflected the districts around the missions La Purísima, Santa Inés, and Santa Barbara, and the island of Santa Cruz, respectively. It is thought that the Gaviota Chumash spoke Barbareño, and the name Quabajai referred to their tribe.

Chumash descendent Juanita Centeno and her collection of Chumash artifacts.

23

The natural world of the Chumash was the source of everything—craft materials, tools, clothing, homes, beds, baskets, money, and food. It was their "department store." No one owned the land—it belonged to all. Local plants provided homes, beds, baskets, and nets. Stone was used for grinding tools, arrowheads, cooking utensils, and knives. Animal hides were used as clothing as well as musical instruments and other belongings. Shells were dishes, ornaments, and currency. An extensive trade system developed among the Chumash, for they traveled long distances on both land and water to exchange commodities with their neighbors.

Chumash apparel was generally made from animal skins, decorated with beads and shells. Sometimes, however, their uniform was simple nakedness. Hair was usually worn long and bound in a pigtail with decorative shells, or coiled in a bun and held in place by a bone skewer. Bodies were heavily painted with red ochre, and each village used a distinct design. Both men and women were tattooed by pricking the skin with cactus spines and rubbing charcoal into the wound.

Chumash villages were known to the Spanish as rancherías, and although some consisted of only a few huts, others were quite large. Each village was ruled by a chief (wot). The Chumash houses (wickiups) were half-dome shaped and varied in size. Willow poles were placed upright around a circle of dug-out earth, bent inward, and tied at the center, leaving an opening for light to enter and smoke to escape. Horizontal poles were lashed to the vertical poles, and grass or tules were layered over the frame. A central stone fireplace provided heat and cooking facilities in inclement weather. Partitions were hung to create rooms, and raised platforms became beds. The doorway was often framed by whalebone vertebrae, from which hung two mats of tules, one of which opened inward, while the other swung outward. If the outside mat closed the doorway, it meant that everyone was gone, while if only the inside mat was closed, this indicated that those present wanted seclusion. An open doorway welcomed visitors.

The Chumash temescal, an underground room with a roof of mud and thatch, was the sweat house—a steam bath. After perspiring, occupants plunged into a nearby stream or the ocean. There were separate cemeteries for men and women, and the Chumash buried their dead in the flexed

A typical Chumash wickiup.

position so that the dead would leave life in the same position in which they had arrived. Treasured items were also put into the graves, and painted poles with personal belongings were placed over the dead. Each ranchería had its own mourners. The Gaviota natives worshiped an invisible spirit, which they thought of as the author of rains, seeds, good health, and luck. Point Conception was their "western gate." It pointed toward the setting sun and was the point of departure from which the souls of the dead left the continent to be with the Great Spirit.

The Chumash of Gaviota were primarily hunters and gatherers, depending on wild plants and animals for their food. Acorns were the staple diet; after repeated washings had leached out the bitter tannic acid, the acorns were ground into a thick mush. Fish were caught with hooks, harpooned, or ensnared in yucca nets. Fowl were shot with arrows or trapped. The Chumash hunted in the Gaviota hills, disguised in a deer skin with antlers still attached and eye holes cut out. Thus the camouflaged "brothers" quietly crept toward a herd until they were close enough to thrust spears into the grazing animals; any animals who escaped could also be shot with arrows by other hunters hidden in the brush.

The Chumash did not wage aggressive warfare or practice scalping. They were a passive people who usually existed in a tranquil atmosphere, but there was feuding between groups, especially in times of scant food supplies. Children lived and worked together with adults. Time was told by the sun, with knots tied in a cord to keep track of the days. Stories transmitted Chumash tradition and culture. Basketry and weaving skills were highly cultivated. Music was part of every ritual and was also "medicine" for the sick. One favorite entertainment was for two male groups to sit next to a fire; a blanket held in the teeth of one team hid the transfer of two sticks, while the other team tried to guess where the sticks were. Musical sounds and rocking added momentum and created tension.

Asphaltum was a fundamental resource, and the Gaviota Chumash had a prime source in their own backyard—an area just east of the beach, later called Alcatraz (pelican) by the Spanish. Small cakes of tar were softened by pressing hot stones against them, and this served as a glue, fastening arrows and spear points on shafts and coating baskets to allow cooking by the repeated addition of hot rocks. Asphaltum was even the Chumash chewing gum.

Tar was very important in canoe (tomol, meaning pine) construction, for which the Chumash were much praised by the Spanish. Segments of driftwood, mostly pine, were "pieced together like a quilt" in different lengths and widths to build this temporary "dwelling" on the ocean. Stone, bone, and shell tools cut, shaped, twisted, and bent planks, fitting them tightly together. Sharkskin sandpapered the hull, and asphaltum glued the segments together and corrected construction mistakes. The canoes were built by the Brotherhood of the Canoe, supervised by the altomolich, and the members of this unique brotherhood were some of the most respected members of their societies. One can almost visualize members of this clique working daily at Gaviota to produce these seaworthy vessels, which were capable of great speed.

The Chumash left part of their legacy in art. Rock paintings have been found among the mountains near Santa Barbara and along the coast near Gaviota, although most of their locations have not been disclosed in order to prevent vandalism. One well-known cave, however, is the "Painted Cave" that lies in a hollow sandstone rock high in the Santa

26

Chumash fishermen set out in a tomol.

An example of Chumash art.

Ynez Mountains and now belongs to the State of California. This cave is protected by an iron gate, installed in 1908 to keep out vandals. The exact message of the vast assortment of images and symbols is not known, but it is felt that they pertain to directions, the passage of time, and that they must have had religious significance. Some observers even feel these designs could have involved evil or supernatural influences. Whatever their true meaning, Chumash art remains to remind us of these indigenous humans who once inhabited this land.

Time and language barriers have contributed to variances and diversities in the knowledge and spelling of the names of Indian villages around the Gaviota Land. There was Amahsik (San Julian), Alalpits ("the hot one," Las Cruces hot springs), Anaupo ("between the cheeks," Las Cruces), Casil (Refugio), Michiw (San Onofre), Lehpew (Cementerio), Kashtayit (Santa Anita), Shisholop (Cojo), and Kunuqaq (Point Conception).

The ranchería at Gaviota itself was Onomgio or Nomingo (also spelled Onomyo, Onomigo, Nomgio, or other similar spellings). This village consisted of over fifty huts, and was the home of about three hundred Chumash. It is thought to have been one of the largest sites along the coast. It was described by the Spanish as "La Gaviota—ranchería of many Indians" (Martinez, 1792). Asiquiyaut is believed to have been its chief. It is not certain on which side of the creek Onomgio existed. Clarence Ruth, an educator and archaeologist who did a lot of excavating, confirmed a village on the east promontory, and highway excavation there revealed a steatite charmstone considered to be one of the finest Chumash artifacts ever found. Rogers believed there was also a Chumash village on the west promontory, perhaps at a different time. The smaller villages at Las Cruces may have been under the jurisdiction of the more important settlement at Gaviota and may have been inhabited on a more temporary basis during hunting and collecting periods.

Although knowledge of the Gaviota rancherías is scarce, it is known that a nearby cave was called husap husahkiw (house of the wind). Mushu (fisherman) was one Chumash at the ranchería. He was a member of the "Twenty," a very special group of men who served as an official council. They lived in different areas and represented various villages. Group meetings were called when necessary.

This was the life of those who lived in the Gaviota Land years ago. Another civilization entered into the existence of these complacent inhabitants in their informal environment, and new names were given to villages and citizens. The land and people were completely altered.

CHAPTER 2

The Spanish Land

The Gaviota Land was to belong to Spain! Control began when Juan Rodriguez Cabrillo was sent to search for a shorter water route between the Atlantic and the Pacific. His two ships, *San Salvador* and *Victoria*, left Navidad, Mexico, on June 27, 1542, to navigate up the Pacific coast, and records were kept to claim the country for Spain. The Chumash sailed out to meet the unknown strangers in "giant canoes." Gaviota was one of Cabrillo's seven anchorages in the Santa Barbara Channel. His two vessels moored there on Tuesday, October 17, 1542. Several sources indicate that the explorers obtained a large quantity of sardines there, and so named the area Las Sardinas, although other information indicates this could have occurred at Goleta. The ships tried to go around Point Conception, which they named Cape Galera because of its resemblance to a ship's galley, but storms drove them back to San Miguel Island (La Posesión) where it is thought that Cabrillo fell and broke his arm. He tried to continue on, but he was compelled to go back to Las Sardinas.

The vessels finally rounded the point and continued their journey up the coast, but other tempests forced their retreat back to San Miguel Island. On January 3, 1543, Cabrillo died from gangrene that developed from his previous injury. Many historians think that he was buried on this island across the channel from Gaviota; others do not agree, however, and Cabrillo's grave has never been located. Nevertheless, agreement seems to be universal that his body does lie somewhere in this area of the Santa Barbara Channel. His chief pilot, Bartolomé Ferrelo, continued the exploration challenge of the coastline, and the ships arrived back at the Port of Navidad, Mexico, on April 14, 1543.

Spanish ships sailed past Gaviota again in 1602, when Sebastian Vizcaíno was sent to reaffirm Spanish claims in California. His three ships, *San Diego*, *Santo Tomas*, and *Tres Reyes*, were to follow Cabrillo's route, and he was to make maps and be on the lookout for anchorages for galleons returning from the Philippines. Often designating locations after the saint's day in which they were observed, Vizcaíno named the harbor of Santa Barbara on December 4 (the feast of Saint Barbara), and this became the name of the city, county, and channel. He also named Point Conception La Concepción as he passed by on December 8 (the feast of the Immaculate Conception). Vizcaíno also discovered and named Monterey Bay, which he described as an excellent port, sheltered from the winds, before he returned to Acapulco on March 22, 1603. The children or grandchildren of the Gaviota Chumash who had seen Cabrillo probably noticed these other unfamiliar ships.

Portolá's Expedition

Spain's next contact with the Gaviota Land was by land instead of by sea. California was now a major Spanish concern, as other countries had become aware of the prosperity of this area, especially the abundant and valuable fur pelts. Alta (upper) California needed to be occupied or it would be lost. Presidios would first be built from San Diego to Monterey for protection, and then missions would follow for religion and conversion of the natives. The bestowal of free land and the founding of towns (pueblos) would also encourage Spanish settlement.

A five-division expedition to San Diego (two by land and three by sea), initiated the possession of California in earnest. Each of these parties traveled separately, to allow for the unexpected. Don Gaspar de Portolá, governor of Baja (lower) California, was in charge, accompanied by the friars Juan Crespi and Junípero Serra, who later became president of the missions. Three ships, *San Carlos*, *San Antonio*, and *San Joseph*, sailed from the assembly point of Loreto, Mexico, on different dates. The *San Joseph* was lost, but the other two arrived at San Diego to combine with the two land groups. Portolá left some members of the expedition at San Diego to establish the first presidio and mission there. Although all four pilgrimages had suffered numerous hardships, and many of the men were ill with

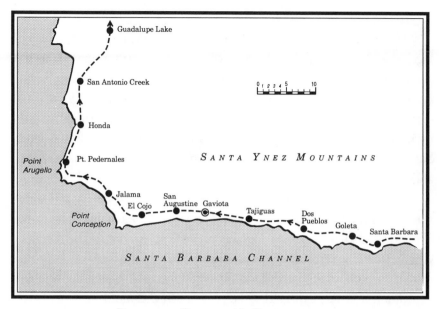

ROUTE OF PORTOLÁ'S EXPEDITION

scurvy, those in the best physical condition combined to travel 600 miles up the coast where no European had gone before.

On July 14, 1769, the half-mile-long column of over sixty men and approximately 100 mules with supplies left San Diego. The expedition frequently followed Indian trails and managed to cover ten to twelve miles per day. Their main objective was to locate the impressive Monterey Bay described by Vizcaíno, which was to become a primary supply port. Careful notes were kept as the expedition surveyed the natives and countryside for occupation. The world-famous exploration gave many permanent names to California landmarks, including Gaviota. The expedition arrived at Carpinteria (carpenter's shop), on the 17th and named it for the canoe construction they saw there by tar pits. The Chumash village at Summerland had already been burned to the ground by Tulare Indians, aggressive neighbors from the San Joaquin Valley who were named for the extensive marshes there. The expedition made camp at Santa Barbara (which they called La Laguna de la Concepción) on the 18th. Ranchería de Mescaltitlan was an island at the time—we now know it as Goleta. The Indians all along the route were friendly to Portolá's party, donating acorns and both fresh and dried fish.

The expedition reached Onomgio at Gaviota on the 24th. The village, located on the bank of the estuary where the river's current meets the sea, contained an estimated 300 Chumash. It was named San Luis Rey de Francia, but after a soldier looking for wood shot a sea gull, the area became permanently known as Gaviota, the Spanish name for the gull. From there, the cordillera of channel islands was prominent: San Miguel, Santa Rosa, and Santa Cruz, known then as San Bernardo, Santa Cruz, and Santa Barbara.

The Spanish had to go up the creek to get fresh water, as salt water washed from the sea into the stream, and there wasn't much firewood. The wind also seemed to "breathe harder" at Gaviota. The Gaviota Chumash had seven canoes for fishing when the party arrived, and some were considered quite large. One Gaviota Chumash joined the Spanish expedition and was expected to be an asset in communicating with the people of other rancherías. Portolá's expedition was significant in the history of the Gaviota Land; it gave the area its permanent name, and a Gaviota native became a guide.

Portolá's company left Gaviota on August 25 and continued along high and rugged country bordering the coast (the present Hollister Ranch). It continued to be windy as they climbed bluffs and went down slopes. The area seemed gloomy, and camps were cold. On August 26 the expedition arrived at the Chumash village of Shisholop, whose chief was lame, and they named it Ranchería del Cojo (village of the cripple). One of Portolá's lame mules was left there, to be reclaimed on the return trip. From Cojo, the party could see Point Conception, where the mountains descended to a point out on the sea. Continuing around the bend of the continent, they headed northward to discover San Francisco Bay, although they failed to recognize Monterey. A second expedition the next year disclosed this prestigious area, and a presidio and mission were founded there.

On the return trip to San Diego, Portolá retraced his route across Santa Barbara County in twelve days. His supplies were waning, and there was now a paucity of food. The Indian villages did not have extra fish to spare; some of the villages had even been deserted. Many of Portolá's men were ill, including Portolá himself, and some had to be transported in hammocks swung between two mules. Holy viaticum was given to three who were believed to be dying. The column stopped to celebrate Mass only twice, once at Gaviota on Sunday, January 7. Portolá reached San Diego January 25, 1770. The expedition had blazed the trail that was to become the link between an eventual twenty-one missions and remains today one of the major traffic arteries of California—El Camino Real, which later developed into the first and one of the most significant highways in the state, U.S. Highway 101.

De Anza's Exploration

For Spain to retain dominion of her "frail California," an overland route from Mexico was necessary. Juan Bautista de Anza, captain of the Tubac Presidio in Sonora, Mexico, was sent to search for the critical route. His scouting party left Sonora on January 9, 1774. It experienced many problems, but it did succeed in locating a mountain pass to coastal California and successfully reached Monterey. De Anza returned to Mexico to convey both soldiers and civilians to the new territory in one of the most massive overland migrations in history. Friar Pedro Font was the expedition's diarist. The group assembled in Tubac; there the Apaches had previously stolen crucially needed horses, and so departure was delayed long enough to obtain replacements. Finally this party of approximately 240 people, including more than 150 women and children, departed in October 1775. They had about 300 head of cattle and 700 horses and mules which carried all the possessions to be had in the new land.

As the explorers traveled along the channel, they saw an estimated 20,000 Chumash (of the Quabajay tribe), one of the largest "societies" they had seen. They reached Carpinteria (or, more probably, Ventura) on February 24, 1776, where they noticed a good mission site (San Buenaventura). In Santa Barbara they bartered for fresh fish. As the exploration got closer to Gaviota, it observed many streams that came down from the hills and a great deal of tar on the beach. Waterspouts were sighted in the ocean, and the fog never seemed to leave. Some thick fogs seemed to come out of the ground. The cortege passed a deserted village just east of Gaviota, where only a cemetery remained, the residents having left after an enemy attack, and they named the site El Cementerio.

The group then descended the slope at Gaviota, traveled on the beach, and the Gaviota Chumash had another encounter with Spanish civilization. De Anza continued west to El Bulito, where boats filled with fish had just returned, and he purchased enough for his party. Proceeding around Point Conception, the expedition continued northward up the coast to finally arrive at Monterey on March 10.

De Anza's expedition was the greatest single movement of settlers during the entire Spanish period and another footprint along El Camino Real. There was now an overland supply route to coastal California, and the successful trek was the turning point for Spanish military protection, mission survival, and colonization.

The Presidios and Missions

Spain could now undertake to organize total conquest of "her" land. Monterey was chosen the capital of California (both Alta and Baja) and became the residence of Governor Felipe de Neve. Presidios were built at San Diego in 1769, at Monterey in 1770, and at San Francisco in 1776; but a fourth presidio was needed to fill the large gap between Monterey and San Diego. This last citadel was established in Santa Barbara on April 21, 1782, and Captain José Francisco Ortega was the first comandante, answering only to the governor, whose authority was the king. The presidio was an outpost in the wilderness, but it was the Spanish church, city, and state. The citadel guarded an enormous area and was accountable for the security of approximately one quarter of California, including Los Angeles. It also guarded the Gaviota Land.

The missions were the most powerful form of Spanish control, and the Santa Barbara Mission (popularly known as the Queen of the Missions) was the first to have influence on the Gaviota ranchería. The chapel was dedicated on December 4, 1786. Temporary buildings were erected, and within a year permanent adobes with tiled roofs were built in a style similar to the presidio. Buildings were arranged around a giant, open quadrangle and surrounded by a thick wall. Approximately 250 Indian adobe homes, each with a door and window, were built nearby. The complex became a self-sustaining community, rich in cattle, hides, and tallow, and

Santa Barbara, Queen of the Missions.

controlled large acreages. There were over 16,500 head of livestock there by 1814, and adobe houses were built in different areas for regional supervision. As the establishment expanded, it gave birth to the beginnings of the city of Santa Barbara.

There were not as many Gaviota converts at the mission, however, as there were from other local areas. Whereas ninety Chumash came from Refugio and sixty-four from Santa Ynez (before the Santa Inés Mission was built), only seventeen came from Onomgio. Some of the Chumash from Gaviota, however, undoubtedly went to the missions at Lompoc and Santa Ynez when they were built, and Comandante Felipe de Goycoechea's records indicate that in 1794 there were only thirty natives remaining at Gaviota.

Another mission site on the coast near Gaviota was considered but rejected; instead, the eleventh original mission, La Purísima Concepción de María Santísima, was founded on December 7, 1787, at the south end of the Lompoc Valley. The mission was later referred to as Mission Vieja (the old mission), since it was destroyed and a replacement was later built at another location.

Restored La Purísima Mission.

The Santa Inés Mission was founded on September 17, 1804, and dedicated in honor of Saint Agnes. This nineteenth mission was established in order to reach some of the Chumash living east of the mountains, and it was also felt that it would be a buffer to the skirmishing Tulares over the mountains. The Tulares attacked other tribes and also shot arrows at Californians imprisoned in the Las Cruces adobe and stole their horses.

The missions' goal was to give the natives religious instruction and teach the Indians the conventions and trades of Western civilization; then the Indians were to be given freedom. The Gaviota Chumash learned to till the soil, raise crops, weave cloth, make soap, produce adobe bricks, and extract hides and tallow from the massive herds of cattle. Children over nine years of age also had assignments. The Indians now lived in permanent adobes (without fireplaces) and were given different clothing and new names. Their new existence was organized into a regimented schedule, and their lives were drastically transformed. Their health was also threatened, as many foreign diseases arrived with the new civilization, and measles, tuberculosis, diphtheria, and other European maladies took enormous tolls of lives. Soon a Chumash birth became a rare event, and the race began dwindling quickly.

The Indians were "rented" out to both civilians and soldiers, with the proceeds going to the missions. When the Spanish government cut off funds in 1810 because of Mexico's revolt, the Chumash became the main source of support for the presidios as well as for the missions. Finally, however, resentment of Spanish abuse exploded on February 21, 1824, when a visiting Chumash was given a brutal lashing at the Santa Inés Mission. Uprisings immediately occurred at the three missions, and there were killings on both sides before the Indians were overpowered. Punishment was instantly meted out. Some Gaviota Chumash undoubtedly witnessed or could have been involved in these revolts. The cause was to have been investigated, but it is not evident that any reforms resulted. The first civil government in Santa Barbara, however, was established in 1824 as a response to the resentment of comprehensive control by the missions and presidios.

The mission system was not intended to be permanent, and secularization began in 1836. Bishops and priests were to replace missionaries, buildings were to become parishes, and the Indians were to have freedom and land. Secularization, however, was the commencement of decline and resulted in abandonment and disintegration of the missions. The Chumash, who had become dependent on others, were not able to assimilate into the new culture, and many retreated inland to band together for survival. Some of them, however, continued to serve as attendants on the developing ranchos, living in huts near the main adobes, and although their former way of life and culture were gone, they performed vital work as ranch hands, gardeners, housekeepers, cooks, and other domestic attendants. Pay was often in food and cloth.

There are no full-blooded Chumash left in the area, but the Santa Ynez Indian Reservation contains residents of partial Chumash heritage. In 1906, the Catholic Church transferred about 100 acres to the United States government for the Indians. As a people, however, the Chumash have literally become extinct. Attempts have been made to reinstate some of their society, but their real story is gone—only fragments are left.

Earthquake of 1812

At a time of political turmoil for the presidios and missions, nature decreed physical destruction as well. One of the most immense earthquakes in channel history occurred, and it is thought that the epicenter was at Gaviota. Both in 1769 and 1770, Portolá's expedition encountered ground tremors that

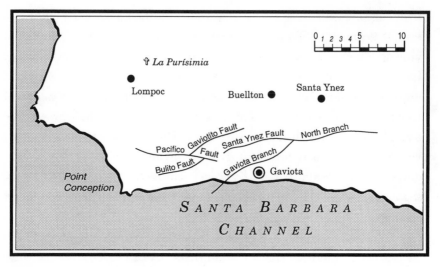

FAULT SYSTEMS AT GAVIOTA

frightened everyone; but the "great one" occurred in 1812. The Spanish called this year "el año de los temblores" (the year of the earthquakes).

There are many seismic faults in the Gaviota Land. The largest of these is the Santa Ynez, whose southern branch rises out of the ocean near the beach at Gaviota and travels northeastward to join its northern branch above Gaviota Pass. The associated faults of Pacifico, Bulito, and Gaviotito are to the west. These faults comprise an energetic system of dangerous magnitude. They are a dominant fault belt in California and have been held responsible for the big earthquake of 1812.

Most of the Chumash had left their villages by the time the quake hit, but those at the missions experienced massive earth agitations. A series of shocks started in May, and a medium-sized temblor occurred on December 8, but the most destructive jolts came on December 21. It was reported that mountains quivered, the earth opened in several places, and sulfur volcanoes erupted. The quake was estimated to have an intensity of from VIII to IX on the Modified Mercalli Scale, or magnitude 8.3 on the Richter scale.

In Cañada Lobo on Santa Rosa Island, a gigantic crack opened up, which was said to be more than one hundred feet deep and fifty feet wide. Immense rocks plunged down the ridges. The Santa Barbara Mission was severely damaged, and presidio roofs were in piles of rubble. At the Santa Inés Mission, the first shock of the destructive quake ripped a hole in the church; the corner fell, and walls cracked. Another agitation flattened the Indian village, but it is not believed anyone was hurt. La Purísima Mission sat right on top of a fault, and during morning Mass the first shock cracked the walls, and another long and furious jolt toppled the church. The mountains split into a huge gully, which is still visible today, emitting water along with black sand, and an unknown number of Chumash were crushed as the entire building collapsed. The mission was a total loss and had to be rebuilt. The new site across the Lompoc Valley was referred to

La Purísima Mission after the 1812 earthquake.

by the Spanish as Cañada de los Berros (little canyon of the watercress).

A tsunami (seismic sea wave) accompanied the earthquake. Such waves can race across the ocean at 600 miles per hour, and their size is related to the quake intensity, the distance traveled, and the underwater geography. A tsunami is often not seen or felt in the open ocean, but as it gets closer to land, a series of waves can swell into a towering wall of water, and its arrival is often preceded by an additional withdrawal of the sea from the shore.

The earthquake of 1812 was associated with the most massive seismic sea wave ever reported in California. The ocean receded a great distance out to sea, then returned in five or six tsunamis, which stormed toward the shore. It is estimated that around fifteen feet of water hit Ventura and from thirty to thirty-five feet struck the coast at Santa Barbara. The mountains of water came in about fifteen-minute intervals, and the terrified inhabitants ran to hilltops to avoid being engulfed by the reappearing ocean waves. Because the sea swept inland at Gaviota, it was calculated that this had been the epicenter of the great quake and a fifty-foot wall of water roared inland, smashing up into the canyon in the Gaviota Land. It was reported that the ship *Mercury*, engaged in illegal sea otter trade and surreptitiously anchored off Refugio, was driven about a mile inland up the canyon by one formidable wave, and another enormous receding wave returned it to the sea.

The aftershocks of this great quake continued for over four months, and the resulting landslides further terrified people. Many abandoned their dwellings to live in the open, and a stick with a pendant ball was used as a measure of seismic movement—one of the first seismological devices ever invented.

CHAPTER 3
Mexican Territory

California and Gaviota were "adopted" by Mexico when that country declared independence from Spain and took her California "child" with her. Spain's manner of control contributed to this. The Spanish crown felt that the colonies existed only for the motherland's gain, and it rigidly governed trade, industry, and religion. Father Miguel Hidalgo y Costilla proclaimed war against Spain on September 16, 1810, but was executed, and Father José Maria Morelos continued the rebellion. Agustin de Iturbide, an army officer, declared Mexican sovereignty in 1821, and a time of political grappling ensued; but the Mexican constitution was ratified in 1824, and Spain was no more to have control of the Gaviota Land.

Bouchard's Raid
During Mexico's revolt, Bouchard's raid on the Ortegas' Refugio Rancho was a principal event in California history, and Gaviota had a part in it. Argentina, which was also rebelling against Spain's rule, sent Captain Hippolyte de Bouchard to attack Spanish vessels and coastal colonies. His two ships, *Argentina* and *Santa Rosa*, had numerous guns and were said to be manned by merciless warriors. The missions and presidios were alerted in October 1818 that these ships were sailing to raze the coast of California, and Bouchard's two frigates arrived in Monterey on November 22. When Governor Pablo Vicente de Sola refused to surrender and retreated, Bouchard landed his force of about 400 men, and left the capital in ruins.

The vessels departed, taking one prisoner with them, and it is believed that Bouchard anchored at Gaviota before his next attack on Refugio, considered an isolated and rich smuggling port where foreign vessels surreptitiously traded. When he landed there December 2, he found that most of the Ortega family had gone to the Santa Inés Mission, taking many of their valuables with them. The rebels vandalized the rancho and killed animals, which included cutting the throats of valuable stallions. Structures were burned, and only charred skeletons of some remained.

Presidio soldiers came to defend the rancho. It is thought they used San Marcos Pass and returned to the coast via Gaviota Pass in order to get behind the enemy; they captured three rebels. Bouchard left Refugio to consider an assault on Santa Barbara, but the appearance of large military strength convinced him not to attack. He was actually tricked: a few men had been marched around to give the impression of massive manpower. Bouchard left the area after prisoners were exchanged. He then tyrannized the San Juan Capistrano Mission before leaving California's coast, but the Refugio raid went down in history.

Smuggling

Spain kept tight control over trade and visiting ships, but a great deal of smuggling went on surreptitiously. The channel's valuable sea otter furs encouraged poaching. Furthermore, because Spanish vessels only came to California about once a year to bring essential supplies, the Californios themselves encouraged secret commerce. Trade restrictions were lifted under Mexican rule, but high tariffs (often 100 percent) made smuggling still necessary, and both ships and settlers encouraged evasion of the full tax. The stopovers of the ships were very important, and life swirled around them.

Usually, vessels unloaded a great deal of their merchandise before declaring their cargo and paying tariffs at the port of entry (usually Monterey). Other times, merchandise was concealed on the ship itself; an immense cache of goods could be hidden inside boat panels, and falsified bills of lading were sometimes used to disguise a ship's cargo; whaling boats were not required to enter custom houses at all, but were allowed several thousand dollars of goods on board to trade for supplies. After the tariffs had been paid, the ships would secretly pick up any cargo they had hidden away, and continued to trade up and down the coast for several years, anchoring in all ports and offshore beach sites where there was an opportu-

nity to procure tallow and hides. Gaviota, Refugio, and Cojo were important illicit trading sites along the channel.

Land Grants

Under Spanish rule, a few small "loans" of land were granted to individuals, usually retiring soldiers, but the land was still considered Spanish. Under Mexican rule, however, large and permanent grants of up to about
48,800 acres were made to citizens in good standing who had properly applied. The grantees were required to build a house, occupy the land, and
stock it. Successful claimants were given deeds, and by the end of the
Mexican period an estimated 700 grants and millions of choice acres had
been distributed. Even former Indian rancherías were not mandated, but
could be included in government land grants.

In Santa Barbara County, approximately forty legal grants were issued
by four Mexican governors between 1834 and 1846. The Treaty of
Guadalupe Hidalgo, signed on February 2, 1848, provided that the legal
rights of Mexican rancheros were to be respected; consequently, the Land
Act of 1851 established a Board of Commissioners to validate all claims of
title. Boundary lines on old charts were often vague or missing, so there
was a great deal of confusion as hundreds of claims were processed in the
next several years. As claims were approved, however, the grants became
legal California properties.

The Gaviota Land was part of the Nuestra Señora del Refugio (Our
Lady of Refuge) grant, considered one of the most important historically.
On some vintage scripts, it is designated "Gaviota." The grant extended
from Refugio almost to Cojo Bay, and included miles of exquisite shoreline. It also contained the natural mountain pass at Gaviota. The 26,529
acres were granted to José Francisco Ortega, a retiring soldier who had
been a sergeant in Portolá's expedition, leader of the reconnaissance group
that discovered San Francisco Bay, and first comandante of the presidio at
Santa Barbara. It was the only land concession granted by Spain in what is
now Santa Barbara County. The title, dated 1786, was really only a grazing permit, reportedly given to allow Ortega to repay a large debt he had
accumulated when he was comandante in Laredo. Ortega died in 1798,
and his sons repaid the debt. Several petitions were made for legal owner-

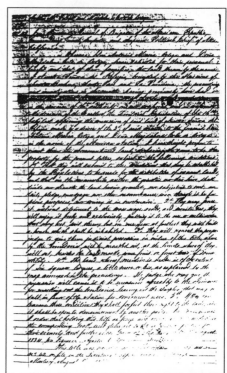

Original land-grant map and description of Nuestra Señora del Refugio.

ship of his land, and there were disputes with mission padres over some areas and boundaries, but grant title was officially vested to Ortega's heirs on August 1, 1834.

Two other grants were important to the Gaviota area. The large San Julian grant of 48,221 acres northwest of the Refugio area was conveyed on April 7, 1837, to José de la Guerra, also a comandante of the Santa Barbara Presidio. By the time of confirmation on September 29, 1873, the ranch belonged to Thomas Dibblee, who had married one of the daughters of Don José, and a part of the history of Gaviota would be linked with that of Rancho San Julian. The Las Cruces area of 8,152 acres was given to Miguel Cordero in 1836 and patented on July 7, 1883. This land was adjacent to the Refugio and San Julian grants, and would eventually become part of the Gaviota Land.

The Point Conception grant of 24,992 acres was allotted to Anastacio

Carrillo on May 10, 1837, and patented on July 13, 1863. This area at the southwestern corner of Santa Barbara County extended from the western end of the Refugio grant, around Point Conception, to Point Arguello. It was later divided into the La Espada (the sword) and El Cojo (the cripple) ranchos. Adjacent to the north of this area was the 42,085 acres of the Lompoc Valley, bestowed to Joaquín and José Carrillo on April 15, 1837, confirmed on November 3, 1873. Immediately to the north was the Mission Vieja grant of 4,413 acres, which was appropriated to the Carrillos on November 28, 1845, and confirmed on November 7, 1873.

Ranchos

Ranchos developed as grants were made. The first homes consisted of mud and logs over an earth floor, but permanent adobe buildings soon replaced them. At the center of each home was the traditional open-air patio, where many daily activities occurred. Gradually the interiors were improved with wooden floors, glass windows, durable furniture, and other amenities. The rancho became a complex of homes for families, foremen (major domos), cowboys (vaqueros), and huts for the Indian servants, who were important for rancho existence. The complex supplied its own needs as much as possible, and luxuries were obtained from trading vessels.

There were always numerous relatives and friends in rancho households in addition to many children, and strangers received gracious hospitality. Cattle multiplied rapidly in the open land without fences. Soon, sizable packs of wild horses roamed over the hills and became a nuisance. They grazed in pastures intended for domestic animals, and when they left, many of the domestic animals followed them. It was sometimes necessary to drive feral stock into corrals for extermination. There were also numerous bears in the area, and sometimes one was lassoed and brought to the rancho to be chained to a bull for a fight to the death of one or both animals.

Rawhide was the currency of the land—a kind of early banknote. A hide was worth from one to two dollars, depending on its quality. Rawhide was indispensable for many uses. It expanded when wet, tightened as it dried, and could be used in numerous ways. Stretched over four wooden poles, it was a bed frame, and interwoven strips made springs. It became a

The carreta, the basic vehicle of Spanish and Mexican California.

rope to lash fences and could be converted into boots, shoes, hats (sombreros), and other leather goods.

Rancho transportation was by horseback or by the crude two-wheeled wooden cart (carreta) pulled by a pair of oxen. The wheels were round sections of tree trunks, and noisy squeaks emitted as they revolved. This early means of travel was slow and tedious and could only be used on relatively flat lands. Horseback was the primary transportation mode, and one animal was usually kept saddled at all times.

The Gaviota Land was part of the Ortega Rancho, which was considered successful and affluent. The main complex was located about a mile up Refugio Canyon. There were approximately 400 fruit trees and 3,000 vinestocks, which made good wine. A dam for water and a grist mill were also part of the headquarters. There were large herds of animals, and crops such as corn, wheat, and beans were cultivated. As the family grew, adobes were built in other canyons as well. One possible such outgrowth was in Gaviota Canyon. Andrea Cota had married Josef Manuel Ortega, and after his death she married Mariano Olivera around 1853. They owned the

Gaviota property from 1858 to 1865, and their home was considered to belong to a wealthy family. There were two adobes, one of two and another of seven rooms. The latter appears to have had asphalt floors, which were quite rare at that time. They also had two hundred seventy-five head of cattle, fifty sheep, and seventy-five horses. The 1860 census listed two Olivera adults and three children at Gaviota, the sixty-third dwelling visited. (Las Cruces was the sixty-second, and Arroyo Hondo was the sixty-fourth.) There were also ten Ortega adults and children.

Hide and tallow trade was an important part of rancho life, and the trade in these items was among the most colorful events of early California life. Great numbers of cattle roamed over the rich and fertile hillsides, and when a ship was known to be coming, there was immense activity to produce hides and tallow for barter. Sometimes vessels even placed orders ahead of time. The cattle were rounded up, brands were separated, and the animals were driven to an area for slaughter (matanza). Riders galloped around to contain them while other vaqueros killed the animals with knives. Quite a few cattle could be killed on the perimeter before the others tried to escape and had to be caught on the run.

After the slaughtered animals were relieved of their skins, the best pieces of meat were used immediately; other meat was dried for jerky. Fresh beef was not part of trade, as refrigeration was not available. The carcasses were left for native predators and scavengers. Fat chunks were dropped into large kettles over hot fires to be turned into tallow, which was poured into holes in the ground for solidification. After the skins were stretched, dried, and folded, they were transported in carretas to the beach, where they were conveyed out to ships, carried high over the men's heads to keep them dry.

After many hides had been collected, they were taken to curing locations, such as San Diego, for preparation and storage before the lengthy journey to the east coast. They were left in large piles near hide houses, and each vessel had its own structure. The skins were staked and soaked in salt water for several days to soften them; then they were stretched on the ground, and any particles were carefully scraped off with a knife. After they were salted, they were placed on racks to dry and later folded, pressed, and flattened for storage. Each hide had to be handled more than twenty times. The ships often operated in pairs; one navigating the coast, exchanging merchandise for hides until it had a full load, then sailing for Boston while the consort ship continued operations in California.

Shelves and glass cases in the ship's showroom displayed the merchandise. The vessels were ocean-going emporiums to the early pioneers. As there were no wharves, small boats carried shoppers to the ships and transferred merchandise to shore. The surf boats had to be carefully navigated to transport passengers and possessions safely. The crew waited for an extra lull in a wave sequence, then ran the boat in with the breakers, riding the crests. The oars were thrown ahead as far as possible during the catapult, and the vessel was quickly dragged to higher ground as soon as it touched shore. Then the customers' "shopping lists" were hauled by Indians back to the ranchos in the slow oxcarts.

Whaling

Whales were important to the economy of the 1800s. Blubber oil provided the world with light; spermaceti, a white fatty ingredient in the head, was used in the production of candles, glycerine, soap, and ointments; ambergris, a waxy matter which brought very high prices, was used in perfumes; and whalebone provided such things as umbrella handles, buggy whips, fishing rods, bustles, corsets, and other articles.

The gray whale is prominent in the channel off the Gaviota Land. The name comes from its color, and tons of barnacles often cling to its skin. These mammals, which breathe air and nurse their young, propel themselves with powerful flukes which can span ten feet. They use baleen to filter out small plankton, crustaceans, and fish from the water. Gray whales do not multiply quickly. Gestation lasts twelve months, and birth is usually every other year. Calves can consume fifty gallons of milk a day to quickly gain the weight and blubber necessary for survival. The young whales weigh approximately one ton at birth and are about sixteen feet long. The mature mammal can weigh well over thirty-five tons and be thirty to fifty feet in length. Whales have to learn most of their adult behavior, and their average life span is about fifty years.

Gray whales spend the summer feeding in the icy arctic seas, then migrate to the warm waters of Baja for breeding and calving. This is the longest known trek regularly made by any mammal on land or sea, at least 10,000 miles, round trip. The journey requires six months or more and is an incredible feat of endurance. The mammals normally cruise in small groups or pods, making four to six miles per hour. They travel outside the channel on their southbound trip in the fall and winter (October to January); on their return journey in the spring (February to April), they swim close to the coastline for the protection of their young.

Whaling stations were located near Goleta and Cojo, and whaling boats were usually dispatched in pairs. Sometimes a lookout on the cliffs signaled the whales' approach. As a whale emerged, a harpoon was fired into its massive body, and the mammal would usually submerge and take off for open sea, towing the boat behind it. When the tired whale surfaced to breathe, an explosive charge was fired, and this might be repeated several times before the whale was finally killed. A buoy on the harpoon helped locate a submerged carcass. When the carcass began to decompose and gasses accumulated, causing it to float to the surface, the whale was dragged to shore, and the blubber was stripped from fat layers. The last of the great mammal was then put into huge iron pots over hot fires to become oil. The remains were left to decompose on the beach, and the atmosphere reeked.

Whalers strip blubber from a whale at Cojo, 1892.

Some of these operations also took place on the whaling ships themselves. Antique cauldrons on board had one flat side to prevent them from rolling and to facilitate storage. Brick fireplaces were built on the decks to extract the whale oil, and the cooled oil was poured into wooden casks to be stored away in the hold. Afterwards, the bloody remains were thrown into the sea.

The whales were greatly reduced in numbers and close to extinction before the market for their oil was replaced by petroleum products, and the whaling industry declined. The International Convention for the Regulation of Whaling, which was ratified by seventeen nations in 1947, the Marine Mammal Protection Act (1972), and the Endangered Species Act (1973) have contributed to restoring these giant mammals.

Although people do not exterminate gray whales as in the past, their natural predator is always a threat to them. Orca (killer whale) attacks are not seen often, but late in one migration cycle (May 1991) two different assaults were recorded. In one onslaught, a pod of seven or more orcas trailed a single female gray with her calf. They charged, rammed, and bit into two-thirds of the mother, who fought to defend her baby. They repeatedly isolated the younger mammal until they could kill it, and it was believed that the mother was so seriously injured that she would also die.

Many petrified whale bones, some millions of years old, have been found off the Gaviota Land from these numerous, graceful "big fish" offshore, and the whales still continue to migrate on the same course and in the same manner.

Petrified whale bone millions of years old, found at Gaviota Beach.

CHAPTER 4

Early Years of Americanization

Mexican Rule Comes to an End—Frémont

Conflict broke out between Mexico and the United States, and the Gaviota Land became the site in California history where a notable ambush did *not* take place. The main dispute was over the southwestern boundary of Texas, which had already been admitted to the United States. The U.S. claimed the border at the Rio Grande, whereas Mexico insisted that the Nueces River, 100 miles eastward, was the border. The first blood was spilled in April 1846, war was declared in May, and the cry of "manifest destiny" was heard over the land. There were four principal fields of action. Lieutenant Colonel John Charles Frémont and Commodore Robert Stockton were in California territory. Frémont had been an explorer, known as the "Pathfinder" for his western frontier maps. He and guide Kit Carson had led an exploration party over the Oregon Trail in 1842.

Most of the fighting took place on Mexican soil, but Frémont played a prominent part in California territory. When the war broke out, Commodore John Sloat raised the U.S. flag at Monterey, proclaiming California part of the United States. He repeated the action in Santa Barbara, where he left a few men under Lieutenant Theodore Talbott. About 200 Mexicans recaptured the town, however, and Talbott's men narrowly escaped. Frémont was dispatched to recapture this lost territory on his way to an anticipated battle in Los Angeles.

Frémont's army of about 500 men was a combination of rangers, frontiersmen, and a few Indians. They didn't have official uniforms, but they were armed with a combination of powder horns, pistols, knives, and rifles;

51

all were considered weapons experts. The battalion desperately needed horses, however. Many had given out, and some men carried their saddles after abandoning lame animals, but the Mexicans had concealed all available animals in the hills.

As Frémont approached the Santa Barbara region, he was expected to use the accustomed route through Gaviota Pass, but he decided that the battalion would turn eastward over the little-known San Marcos trail in order to arrive at Santa Barbara's "back door." The Gaviota ambush story relates that an English-born Mexican citizen, Benjamin Foxen, warned Frémont of the planned attack in the pass. Men on top of the lofty cliffs would roll down boulders, and surviving soldiers would be shot as they tried to escape.

Although this story has been repeated for generations, there are some reasons to doubt its authenticity. The ambush warning is not documented, and most of the available Mexican males are thought to have been fighting in a major confrontation in Los Angeles, although it is thought that Frémont did not realize this until he arrived in Santa Barbara. It was also the rainy season, and Gaviota Creek could have been a raging river. Furthermore, it is also not considered probable that the narrow opening of the pass would have allowed the passage of wagons and cannons.

The reason that Frémont deviated from the regular route is not known, but surprise and the need for horses were involved. His officers, however, feared danger to both men and animals in trying to attempt an unknown mountain course. The battalion proceeded over the obscure bridle path around Christmas, 1846, and history indicates that the guides were Benjamin Foxen and his son, William, although a Romero has also been mentioned.

Brush had to be slashed, rocks moved, and wagons and cannon had to be dangled in sections across ravines. As the troops started downward on precipitous grades, the weather became more severe. The sky was smothered by menacing clouds, and heavy rains drenched men and animals as they slid down vertical hillsides. Shrubs and trees were uprooted, and boulders rolled down the steep slopes. Cannon had to be abandoned and other equipment jettisoned, and it is estimated that about 100 animals were lost.

The exhausted battalion finally reached the bottom and tried to keep warm in wet blankets. After the downpour ceased December 26, lost members were located, surviving animals were collected, and deserted equipment was brought down. Browsing steers were killed for food, and the army marched into Santa Barbara to hoist permanently the American flag. Frémont's battalion remained there until January 3, 1847, then continued on to Los Angeles to join Stockton and others in battle.

Frémont and General Andres Pico signed the Cahuenga Articles of Capitulation on January 13, ending the war, and California and the Gaviota Land formally became American territory with the signing of the Treaty of Guadalupe Hidalgo on February 2, 1848. Prisoners on both sides were to be released immediately, arms and artillery were to be surrendered, and equal rights and privileges of citizenship were to be provided for all. An area of more than 525,000 square miles was added to the United States, and the Rio Grande was confirmed as the southwestern boundary of Texas. The United States gave Mexico $15 million and paid the claims of American citizens against the Mexican government. The city of Santa Barbara began its legal existence on April 9, 1850, and California became the 31st state on September 9, 1850. Mexican control in California was over, and a new era inaugurated.

Plaque commemorating an ambush that never happened.

No one will ever know what would have happened if Frémont had proceeded over his anticipated route through Gaviota Pass. Even though the threat of ambush may not have been real, today in the pass (and also in Foxen Canyon and at San Marcos summit) stands a monument to this time in history. The monument has been moved several times during highway construction. It was initially placed near the "face of the Indian" in the original two-lane highway (deeded as a public park by John James "J.J." or "Jim" Hollister). It was then shifted to a south lane pull-off near the pass and finally transferred to the northbound rest area where it remains as a reminder of that time in history.

Bandits

Although it had become part of the United States, California was without a government until a constitutional convention was convened at Monterey on September 1, 1849. The state constitution was signed on October 13, and a governor and members of the legislature were chosen. An act subdividing the state into counties and appointing county seats was approved on February 18, 1850. Section 4 of that act created Santa Barbara County, which included the Gaviota Land. It was then a massive district stretching from Los Angeles County to San Luis Obispo County.

Following statehood, thousands of settlers came to California to get rich after gold was discovered near Sutter's Fort in 1848. Caravans from Mexico and others en route traveled along the coast, crossing through Gaviota Pass, which was then open only in good weather to those on foot. No large gold strikes were made in the Gaviota Land, but discoveries in other parts of California affected the area in another way. Thus far, the rancheros had marketed only hides and tallow, leaving the rest of the cattle to decompose; now, even larger profits could be made by selling the meat to prosperous but famished miners. Large herds were soon being driven to the gold-rush country to take advantage of this lucrative market.

Men returning on lonely trails from the mines with precious gold dust were easy prey for bandits, especially if they were traveling alone or in small groups. Some simply disappeared and were never heard of again. Human skeletons with bullet holes in their skulls were often found in the brush alongside the road. The road between Santa Barbara and San Luis

Obispo was considered extremely dangerous and could be a death trap for the unguarded. A gulch near Santa Ynez was named La Cañada de Calaveras (Skull Canyon) because of the numerous remains found there. Any stranger was regarded with suspicion. Travelers rode on open roads only in daytime and even then went as quickly as possible through certain sections. The isolated mountain passes in Santa Barbara County were favorite haunts of bandits, and Gaviota Pass was one of the loneliest spots of all.

Salsipuedes got its name in bandit days, when a group of cattlemen returning from San Francisco with gold had to ride through a narrow canyon as they got near Rancho San Julian. Suddenly, a band of outlaws appeared, shut them off, and trapped them in the canyon. The bandits shouted "¡Sal si puedes!" ("Come out if you can!") while waiting for their surrender. The men had to part with either their wealth or their health.

Joaquín Murrieta. Violence and lawlessness were widespread, and some of the most famous robbers and murderers in California operated in this area. Joaquín Murrieta (Murrietta, Murietta) was one of the most fearless, and one of his hideouts was reported to be in the adobe in Arroyo Hondo (deep creek), not far from Gaviota. Considerable material has been written about this notorious bandit, but it is likely that there was more than one person who committed the myriad of crimes attributed to him. Murrieta's gang had a signal which identified friends along the trails and on the ranchos: three fingers widely spread, with the thumb and little finger closed, used in any natural way.

Murrieta was killed by a group of about twenty men who were formed to wipe out desperado gangs—the Rangers, led by Captain Harry Love. They ambushed Murrieta in a canyon near Coalinga in 1853, and, so the story goes, beheaded him. His head is said to have been preserved in alcohol in order to give proof of death for the $1,000 bounty.

Murrieta's operations in Santa Barbara County often occurred near the coast, and some legends of his plunder were said to have occurred in the Gaviota Land. It is thought that he buried loot in some caves in Gaviota Pass. There is also a rumor of treasure buried in the canyon at Las Cruces, under an oak tree located near a rock with a cross carved on it.

Another story told of the gang's demands for cattle-sale money at Las Cruces. After Murrieta brutally ripped off a señora's earrings, she told him in pain and fright that the money was hidden under a certain tree. This spot is thought to have later become a bandit rendezvous. Yet another tale tells how a Santa Ynez Chumash took Murrieta and his band to his hut, where they coldbloodedly killed the Indian and his family. Their throats were slashed, and the structure was burned to the ground to conceal the crime.

Salomon Pico—El Zorro. Another of the infamous bandits was Salomon Pico, an expert horseman and a native of the Santa Barbara area, which was the center of his operations. He was a cousin to both Governor Pio Pico and General Andres Pico, who surrendered to Frémont at Cahuenga Pass. When gold was discovered near Salomon's Sierra Nevada foothill rancho, crimes were committed against his family and property. It was said that his crops were stolen, his livestock slaughtered, and that his wife died after being raped. Having thus lost all he owned, Salomon felt justified in robbing and killing foreigners, giving much of the stolen gold to friends and relatives.

Because Salomon was from an old, respected family, he was protected by his countrymen. He played a dual role—a respected citizen by day and a highwayman by night. Taking gold from his enemies (rich miners and cattle buyers) and giving it to others was a little like Robin Hood, and he became immortalized as "El Zorro" (the fox), who robbed the rich to feed the poor. He often camped northwest of Los Alamos, where the Solomon Hills (Jewish spelling) were named after him. No one knows just how he died, but when he disappeared and faded from history, a man by the name of Jack Powers took over the remainder of his men.

Jack Powers. Jack Powers was one of the most notorious bandits of old California, and he, too, made the Santa Barbara area the center of his operations. This good-looking, six-foot-tall man mingled with the elite of society, but he was also a professional gambler and bandit leader. He had come from Ireland, joined the Army, mustered out of the Stevenson Regiment in Santa Barbara in 1848, and became the De la Guerra stable caretaker, a position that made him privy to information on cash livestock transactions. Powers preyed on gold miners traveling El Camino Real, and a large number of human skeletons buried in shallow graves in this area are considered to be Jack Powers' victims. Down the beach to the east of Gaviota is "three-fingers Jack's cave." It is not known which "Jack" used this rocky hideout, but if Powers continued to use the Murrieta hand signal, it is likely that this name refers to him.

Suspicion finally fell on Powers, but his alibi was the impossibility of one man traveling the distances involved so quickly. It was later learned, however, that Powers had fresh horses stationed along the way. After he was exposed, he absconded with most of his gang, heading for Mexico. It was thought that he had a ranch there stocked with stolen cattle, and it was rumored that he quarreled with another gang member over a woman and was murdered.

Judge Edward McGowan

Powers was considered one of the worst outlaws in California, but he was also known for his association in 1856 with Judge Edward McGowan, a fugitive from vigilantes in San Francisco.

James King, editor of the San Francisco *Evening Bulletin*, was a supporter of the Vigilante Committee, a group of about 6,000 San Francisco citizens who wanted to take the law into their own hands to eradicate criminals. When King disclosed that James Casey, rival editor of the San Francisco *Sunday Times*, had been in Sing-Sing Penitentiary in New York for felony, Casey shot King with McGowan's gun. After a trial in a kangaroo court, Casey was taken out of jail by the vigilantes and hanged.

McGowan was implicated by the weapon, and rewards were put out for his capture. He disguised himself as a friar, staining his face and dyeing his hair and mustache. He and a companion, James Dennison, left San Francisco at night to travel El Camino Real to Mexico, but they only got a short distance past Gaviota. McGowan thought it was now safe to take off his disguise, but he was recognized by a San Francisco judge in Santa Barbara, and it was none other than Jack Powers who helped McGowan escape from the sheriff's posse. He rolled the plump judge up in an old carpet and told others that the judge had gone. Fires were set to flush him out of

The narrow trail over Gaviota Pass was the perfect place for an ambush.

the brush, and a house-to-house search was made. McGowan was miserable, extremely thirsty, bitten by massive, ravenous fleas, and felt he was going to die from suffocation, but he was not discovered.

A reward was offered for McGowan's capture, and vigilantes searched the countryside, but they did not find him. He stayed in open country, at the Pedro Ortega adobe in Arroyo Hondo, east of Gaviota, and in the cornfield of Don Nicolas Den. Finally he was able to return to San Francisco to win an acquittal and publish an anti-vigilante book.

McGowan was one of the first Americans to comment on Gaviota Pass. He thought the region was wild and remote. Nature seemed to have constructed it just for an ambush, and McGowan was afraid of getting trapped there. When he and his companion were going to travel through the area, they left late in the day to avoid being seen, and before reaching the pass they stopped to dismount and tighten their saddles. After listening to the ground for any sounds or vibrations from other horsemen, they were extra cautious as they rushed through the mountain crevice.

The "gate" of Gaviota Pass. Note the Indian head formation.

First State Geological Survey—Brewer

The Gaviota Land was part of the first state geological survey. Gold discoveries stimulated an acute interest in the location of minerals, and the Act of April 21, 1860, authorized a scientific survey of the state's geology. William H. Brewer, assistant to the state geologist, was to accurately record observations made in California between 1860-1864.

The survey party left Southern California in December 1860. They traveled over dirt roads, high hills, and deep canyons, taking careful notes. Some of the roads were scarcely detectable trails, but others the party considered well-designed. The local thoroughfare was traveled more than others. Small groups of five to ten riders passed by on horseback, pulling pack mules with baggage, and they could ride sixty miles a day or more. Many of the women had black hats with feathers and colorful dresses as they rode sidesaddle with a strap holding them down.

The Santa Barbara area had long been nearly isolated by the rugged mountains and had been accessible only by what was called an "awful trail"; but the survey found that the county had recently spent money for a "good wagon road" that would provide dependable transportation from San Luis

Obispo to Los Angeles as soon as the southern portion of the road was completed. The road included wooden bridges—the first seen in the area—and the animals were nervous crossing them. It was spring, and the mountains were radiant with wildflowers, while massive herds of cattle, horses, and sheep grazed in green fields of grass. A mastodon tooth was found along the way—a memento from a former resident.

The survey saw the first Overland Stage from San Francisco arrive in Santa Barbara on April 1, 1861. The mountains west of Santa Barbara lay close to the sea, and the only break in them was at Gaviota Pass, a crevice that divided the ridge. The narrowest part of the "gate" was only a few feet wide, and towering cliffs soared up on both sides. The road continued to wind up through the "wildest" pass the surveyors had yet seen, and after climbing for about six miles to the summit, they made camp at Nojoqui (camp #21) on Thursday, April 4. Professor Brewer and another member of the survey did not agree on the geology of the Gaviota Pass and returned the next day to go through it again. They climbed up the lofty hills, where there was a beautiful panorama of the ocean. They found fossils in the area, and a rattlesnake met its death at their hands.

The survey was a disappointment to some people, but it was also considered valuable in many respects. It furnished information to be used later, and the remote Gaviota Land was included in the first comprehensive study of the physical structure of California.

Some Extreme Weather

The Simoon. Although not much had previously been written about weather, a rare occurrence at Gaviota and the adjoining areas of the channel went down in the records on June 17, 1859. On an unusually warm day, a scalding wind came from the northwest in the early afternoon. A United States Coast Survey vessel recorded a temperature of 133° at 2 P.M. It was a simoon! After several hours, the heat "cooled" to 122°. People hid in adobes to escape the outdoor broiler. Fruit fell from trees and shriveled on the ground. Crops were destroyed. The hot blast killed small animals, birds lay dead, and even mature cattle perished under oak trees. The coast from near Ventura to Gaviota experienced the only simoon then recorded in American history. It was hot that day!

Another smaller event at Gaviota (and Anaheim Landing) went down in the records of the late 1870s. A small tsunami was noted as the incoming tide suddenly rose five feet in just a few minutes. The high water tossed and churned, then was suddenly sucked back out to sea again. The rapid rush back, however, left fish and other sea life floundering in the sand, waiting for normal tides to return them to deep water.

Heavy Rains and Drought of 1861-1864. The heavy rains of 1861-1862 also went down in history. The exact amount of rainfall is not known, for accurate rainfall measurements were not yet made, but drastic changes occurred in the land. Swollen rivers pulled up vegetation and uprooted trees. Cattle drowned in floods, and land slippages occurred in many places. Gaviota Creek was a rampaging river. Landslides occurred on the pass, and the road was entirely washed away in places.

After two years of massive rainfall, the next two brought a serious drought (1863-1864). It is estimated that less than four inches of rain fell in that time, and this was disastrous. Streams dried up, and springs disappeared. The green hills of the rainy years and high prices commanded in cattle sales had resulted in overstocked ranges, and all available grass was quickly eaten or died. There were no railroads to bring in feed or to transport animals out, so weak ones fell on the hillsides, dying by the hundreds. They were too feeble to be driven elsewhere. Thousands of carcasses lay on the plains, some in heaps around dried-up water holes, and they became meals for scavengers.

Majestic, old oak trees were cut down so that cattle could eat the foliage, although this did not provide sufficient nourishment. Slaughters were held to salvage hides. With overstocked herds and little food, it was even reported that animals were driven over cliffs, to become a shark smorgasbord. In the county, an estimated 300,000 head of cattle shrank to about 5,000. Horse herds were also victims of the drought, and roundups were organized to kill wild, unbranded stock to save feed for domestic animals.

The cattle industry never recovered. Owners became delinquent on taxes and bills; debts mounted. The once-large ranchos were broken up, and ownership passed into other hands as forced sales were made at low prices or acres were mortgaged and lost through foreclosure. This changed the land forever.

Two types of stages in common use: the fancy Concord and the basic but practical "mudwagon."

CHAPTER 5

Stagecoach Days

The Stages

Some of the stagecoaches in the Gaviota Land were Concords—so called because they were built in Concord, New Hampshire, by the Abbott & Downing wagon factory. The Concord had seating for three adults on each side and a jump seat in the center for additional passengers. Others could ride on top. The vehicles, which cost approximately $1,500, were quite tall and weighed about 2,500 pounds. The body was slung on strap springs to help absorb shocks, but roads were rugged, and passengers bounced up and down on the hard seats. If drivers followed dry stream beds in summer, the jolting was even more severe. Most of the stages rolling by Gaviota, however, were "mudwagons." They were not as graceful looking but were built more sturdily to better handle the difficult mountain roads. They were slung on thoroughbraces, weighed less, and were lower to the ground to reduce the risk of overturning.

The teams generally consisted of four or six horses. The lead animals were lighter and specially trained to be surefooted and quick in response. The center, medium-sized animals were the "swingers," while those next to the vehicle were the "wheelers"—the heavy pullers. Four-horse teams were without the middle animals; sometimes mules were also used. The stages traveled as much as possible during daylight hours. They had oil-burning lamps on either side, which provided small illumination at night, but night vision and reaction depended on the animals.

Stages on the lonely roads were easy prey for bandits, and Gaviota Pass was known for being narrow and isolated. Drivers always had to reckon with the possibility of a holdup. Company policy did not encourage drivers to fight or shoot, however, for fear that this could cause runaways, a possible wreck, the loss of valuable stage property or lives. The safe under the driver's seat was locked with a heavy iron ring and could only be opened by station keys. To force it open required two bandits—one to beat open the box while another kept the passengers at gunpoint.

Although stagecoach days are considered some of the most colorful in history, passengers were subjected to long hours of travel on dusty roads, unavoidable delays, and the possibility of being overturned or robbed, and they were quite fatigued by the time they reached their destinations. Women stage travelers rarely spoke except to a friend or neighbor and could make an entire trip without conversation, but the vociferous men often told yarns. To make things go as smoothly as possible, certain rules were posted.

TEN COMMANDMENTS FOR STAGE PASSENGERS
Adherence to the following rules will insure a pleasant trip:

1. Abstinence from liquor is preferred. If you must drink, share the bottle. To do otherwise makes you appear selfish. And don't overlook the driver.
2. If ladies are present, gentlemen are urged to forego smoking cigars and pipes, as the odor of same is repugnant to the weaker sex. Chewing tobacco is permitted, if you spit *with* the wind, not against it.
3. Gentlemen passengers must refrain from the use of rough language in the presence of ladies and children. This rule does not apply to the driver, whose team may not be able to understand genteel language.
4. Robes are provided for your comfort during cold or wet weather. Hogging robes will not be tolerated. The offender will be obliged to ride outside with the driver.
5. Snoring is disgusting. If you sleep, sleep quietly.
6. Don't use your fellow passenger's shoulder for a pillow. He or she may not understand, and friction could result.

A *wagon trudges over Gaviota Pass*.

7. Firearms may be kept on your person for use in emergencies. Do not discharge them for pleasure or shoot at wild animals along the roadside. The noise riles the horses.
8. In the event of a runaway, remain calm. Jumping from the coach may kill or injure you or leave you at the mercy of the elements, highwaymen, and coyotes.
9. Topics of discussion to be avoided have to do with religion, politics, and above all, stagecoach robbery or accidents.
10. Gentlemen guilty of unchivalrous behavior toward lady passengers will be put off the stage. It is a long walk back to Santa Barbara. A word to the wise is sufficient.

Roads, Routes, and Stations

The county road enabled stages to roll through the Gaviota Land. The road went from Los Angeles County to the beach at Rincon, through Carpinteria, Santa Barbara, Goleta, and Dos Pueblos, turning at the Gaviota Pass to continue on to Las Cruces, Nojoqui, Santa Inés Mission, Foxen Canyon, and Santa Maria at Suey Crossing, near the San Luis Obispo County line. This first stage route through the county would often be referred to as the "Gaviota Pass Road." The northern portion was finished, and the southern section toward Los Angeles was nearing comple-

EARLY STAGE ROUTES THROUGH THE GAVIOTA LAND

tion when the first "down" stage from San Francisco went through Gaviota Pass and on to Santa Barbara on April 1, 1861. (Stages went either "up" or "down" California.) Cannons were fired in celebration, and it was considered a big day.

When the Santa Ynez Turnpike Road was constructed by Chinese labor over San Marcos Pass in 1868, it was the second stage route over the challenging Santa Ynez Mountains. This toll road competed with the Gaviota Pass Road, and stages then used both routes. Several stage owners favored the milder incline over Gaviota which required fewer horses. Flint and Bixby Company assumed ownership of the Overland Mail Company in 1868 and used the San Marcos Pass, and for several years the company bypassed the post office at Las Cruces, breaching its contract. Records revealed that no mail came into or went out of Las Cruces during that time. Other stages using San Marcos Pass began to travel the easier Gaviota Pass grade in 1889, when mail was re-routed.

Stage stations changed constantly. Stops were placed at intervals that would allow the horses to travel at a good gallop; depending on the terrain, this was about sixteen miles. When the horses were changed, the coach and driver could be switched also; the passengers, mail, and other freight were merely transferred to another vehicle. There was often a blacksmith shop at the station, because the rough travel quickly deteriorated the shoes of the horses. Meals were served at many stations, while others only had a stove for passengers to prepare their own nourishment. Drivers earned approximately $125 a month, and their meals and lodging were generally free—in fact, it was considered an honor to a hotel owner for the driver to stay at his lodging.

Passengers were sometimes asked to walk part of the way. This happened in June 1864, when "all hands walked for a distance" through the Gaviota Pass. The mountains, however, were noted for their "grandeur." Stage passage through the pass was also difficult during inclement weather. Slides and heavy rains were always a threat at the pass. In May 1862, roads were entirely washed away. The Overland Mail had to suspend services for weeks, and mail was again sent by steamers. In February 1869, the Los Angeles *Star* reported that the Gaviota Pass road had again been obliterated, and mail had to be carried on men's shoulders for a long distance in order to connect with stages on each side. It was thought that it would be some time before the road would be in "passable order."

Stagecoach accidents could happen, and one occurred east of Gaviota at Naples in March 1893. The stage driver tried to cross a high creek when passengers were afraid of missing a Gaviota steamer. The lead horses drowned when their harness caught in willow trees, but the driver saved the others. The passengers jumped from the half-submerged coach, and all reached shore except one man of Chinese descent whose body was never found. They must have missed the steamer, however.

La Graciosa (near the present site of Orcutt) was one station on the changing routes. Another, at Naples, was composed of a stage barn and a hotel with eating facilities. Childs Station (named after the Buellton postmaster) was at the junction of the Gaviota Pass route and the Santa Ynez River. William Ballard built an inn called The Adobes in 1865 in the Santa Ynez area. In the 1880s, Ballard's station was superseded by Mattei's Tavern in Los Olivos. Two stage lines from there went to Santa

Barbara; one went through Nojoqui, Las Cruces, and over Gaviota Pass, and the other used San Marcos Pass.

There was a relay station at Arroyo Hondo, where meals were served. Another adobe station was at Rancho San Julian, where passengers could eat and spend the night. While most former stage stops are gone, there is one existing adobe today in the Buellton area, which some old timers have been "told" was a stage stop (the Flanagan adobe). It was not an official stopover, but stages and travelers would sometimes stay at private homes, and possibly this may be the case. The Flanagan adobe belongs to Benjamin Debolt and Gertrude (DeBolt) Burmester and is one of the few extant adobes and an example of their construction. Another existing adobe is the crumbling former Las Cruces stage stop. It was an official station, hotel, store, saloon, and restaurant, located at the confluence of both streams and crossroads of routes. From there, travelers went west to Lompoc through Rancho San Julian, north to Nojoqui, or south through the Gaviota Pass to Santa Barbara.

There were many feeder lines to the main route between San Francisco and Los Angeles. Rucker Stage made regular trips from Lompoc to Gaviota. The Wines Stage Company ran between Santa Barbara and

Flanagan adobe.

Former Las Cruces stage stop.

Wagons at the Lompoc stage stop, en route to and from Gaviota.

Jim Meyers drove the Lompoc to Gaviota Stage (1894).

Lompoc, changing at Gaviota. Swanson's Livery Stable in Lompoc was a headquarters, and Jim Meyers was a driver for many years on this line. The old Lompoc Hotel was a stage stop until it burned in 1893. Saunders' Stage was noted in 1889 as making daily connections from Lompoc to Gaviota, meeting steamers going north and south:

In 1891, the Lompoc Stables (Talbott Brothers, proprietors) met stage needs:

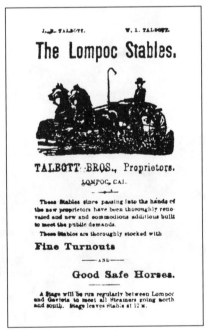

Foundations of Olivera adobe.

For many years, the road from Lompoc to Gaviota through Rancho San Julian had gates which had to be kept closed to prevent cattle from straying, and it was necessary for drivers to open and close them. But for at least one twenty-four-hour period every year, usually in inclement weather, the gate remained locked. This prevented a private road from becoming a public highway. According to the law of that time, if public conveyances used such a byway for 365 consecutive days, it became a public thoroughfare. In later years, however, the road became state Highway l.

Gaviota was considered a main stage stop between 1861 and 1864, and Andrea (née Cota) and Mariano Olivera's adobe in the canyon may have been the station. Two foundations were discovered in 1987 under three feet of ground, and it is speculated that a massive slide from heavy rains may have been responsible for their burial. Miguel Burke is known to have been in the Gaviota Land in 1875, when the wharf was built. His adobe was close to the mouth of Gaviota Canyon, where he was wharfmaster and operator of a feeder stage line over Gaviota Pass between Las Cruces and Santa Barbara, later extended to Ballard's station (The Adobes) in Santa Ynez and Guadalupe. His available accommodations and services at the mouth of the Gaviota Canyon were:

M. F. BURKE
Proprietor of
GAVIOTA STORE AND HOTEL
Dry Goods, Groceries
Provisions, Boots, Shoes
Cigars, Tobaccos, Wines, Liquors
Hardware, Tinware
Willow Goods, Glass and Crockeryware, etc.
Hotel well furnished.
Table and sleeping apartments unexceptionable
Proprietor of
STAGE LINE FROM LAS CRUCES TO SANTA BARBARA
Also, Manager of Gaviota Wharf
Where will be found good shipping facilities.
Western Union Telegraph Office at the Store

Burke also had 700 sheep, 100 head of cattle, and 30 horses at Gaviota. (In this period it was also recorded that the Selby orchard near Gaviota contained around 500 acres of fruit trees.)

Burke was appointed a county supervisor in 1882, and Henry Edward McNealy (also spelled MacNeally or McNeely) replaced him at the Gaviota Adobe Inn for stage and steamer passengers until around 1902. (He formerly had a grocery store at H Street and Ocean Avenue in Lompoc.) Henry and his wife, Maria, had twelve children. His daughter, Amy, was the first official postmaster at Gaviota from April 23, 1896 to January 31, 1901, when the mail was forwarded to Alcatraz after the railroad gap was closed. Amy married Henry Ramsey, and they also managed the Gaviota Adobe Inn. In later years the inn was covered over by highway construction, where it remains under a huge mound of dirt. (It was later dubbed the "Peppers Adobe" for the nearby pepper trees.)

A team prepares to leave the Las Cruces stage stop.

Las Cruces Murder

There was strong competition for the profitable stagecoach business. When a proposal was made in 1864 to move the stage stop from Gaviota to Las Cruces, two murders were committed in anticipation of the relocation. Wilson and Lucretia Corliss built a new house a short distance from the Las Cruces crossroads in order to get the enterprise, and they were beaten, killed, and locked inside the structure, which was then burned. Francisco Coronado, a shepherd living with them, was also found dead several weeks later, his body crammed between some rocks.

It was necessary to know which of the Corlisses had died first, since they had both been married before, and the children of the last spouse alive would receive all of the inheritance. The wife was found over the husband on the hearth. Sheriff R.J. Broughton concluded that Wilson had died first from an intense blow to the head. Marks found in the garden where Lucretia had first struggled indicated that she had been the last one alive.

The murder caused an uproar in Santa Barbara, and a vigilante committee was formed to assist the sheriff in apprehending the killers. One group hid in a stage which went to Gaviota, where they arrested at least one family member who was a suspected "desperado." Another group came later to pick up any "questionable characters" along the road.

The Williams brothers from Oregon, Bill, Elize, and Steve, became prime suspects, for they had made improvements to the Cordero adobe at Las Cruces in anticipation of getting the stage business. A Mexican woman also confirmed that the brothers had offered to pay her to put strychnine in milk delivered to the Corlisses. The Williamses were arraigned in court but released after a lengthy trial because of the lack of concrete evidence.

Bill went back to Oregon, and Elize and Steve continued to live at the Las Cruces stage station, but they had to move their sheep in the drought of 1864. They were found murdered near San Luis Obispo, and a hired man was hanged when he was found wearing one of their watches. Their fourth brother, Bascomb, arrived in 1865 to probe into their deaths. He later took charge of the adobe inn and also served as postmaster, deputy sheriff, constable and justice of the peace.

After March 31, 1901, when the Southern Pacific railroad was completed along the coast, forty years of stagecoaching ended. The mail then went by rail. Felix Mattei, however, maintained a twice-weekly stage service from Los Olivos and Solvang to Gaviota, which was then the only way to get to Santa Barbara for those in the north. Passengers left Los Olivos early in the morning for the Gaviota depot in order to take a train out at 6 P.M. Mattei's stages ran until around 1914, and those vehicles rocking and swaying to Gaviota may have been some of the last stagecoaches in the United States.

CHAPTER 6

The Hollister-Dibblee Empire and the Gaviota Wharf

The Partnership

Colonel William Welles Hollister, an influential citizen whose family owned a large part of the Gaviota Land for many years, became part of Gaviota's history when the Hollister-Dibblee partnership was formed. Hollister was from Hanover, Ohio, born January 12, 1818, next to the last of five children. The rank of Colonel came from the Hanover Volunteers, a home guard unit. Hollister had been a horticulture major in college, and after his father died, he and his brother, Joseph "Hub" Hubbard, managed the family farm of more than 1,000 acres, plus the village store, a sawmill, an iron furnace, and a gristmill. Hollister heard about the large cattle profits being made in the California mine fields and drove a herd out from Ohio in 1852. While waiting weeks for return passage on booked-out steamers, he observed the large numbers of plump sheep grazing in the fertile hills ; he decided to return to California with prime merino stock, becoming one of the first to drive sheep across the continent.

Financial assistance came from Hollister's sister, Lucy Brown, who had an inheritance from her deceased husband. A large crowd of the Ohio town's residents watched Hollister, Hubbard, and Brown set out in 1853 to head for Monterey County. Their party took about six thousand sheep, fifty shepherds, and fifteen supply wagons. During the long journey there were many hardships, such as lack of water, severe weather, and Indians. Many sheep were lost along the way in quicksand, or died from eating poisonous plants or from sheer exhaustion. Many of the animals' feet wore out, preventing them from getting food, and so they starved.

The Hollisters' large drive joined forces with another sheep herd driven by Dr. Thomas Flint and Llewellyn Bixby. When the two groups separated, Hollister continued past the Gaviota Land and on up the coast. When he arrived at his destination, fifteen months after his departure, he had only about a thousand sheep, but his venture was successful, and he joined Flint and Bixby in the purchase of the San Justo Ranch near the present town of Hollister. When the ranch was later sold, Hollister used the money for land purchases in the Santa Barbara area, in partnership with Albert and Thomas Dibblee.

Albert Dibblee came to San Francisco in 1848 to handle shipping to the east coast. He then went into partnership with William Corbitt to purchase the 15,600-acre Santa Anita Ranch near Pasadena, which his lawyer brother, Thomas, later managed. The Hollister-Dibblee partnership was formed after a meeting at Zaca Creek Ranch. Hubbard, Joseph Cooper, and Colonel Newton Peters had also driven sheep west, and when Peters died, Hubbard and William Hollister, Joseph Cooper, and Albert and Thomas Dibblee met at his ranch to buy his merino stock. The group got together to purchase the Lompoc Ranch for $60,000. William had one third; Albert and Thomas shared a third, and Joseph and Hubbard shared another third. The Lompoc Ranch was later sold after cockleburs and Mexican thistles spread over the land, as these were difficult to remove from the wool.

Hubbard and Joseph purchased the 15,512-acre Santa Rosa Ranch in the Santa Ynez Valley, and William Hollister and Thomas and Albert Dibblee formed their famed partnership. Hollister was a principal financier. Albert negotiated wool prices and handled shipments in San Francisco. Thomas was the overseer, and George Long, who had managed the Santa Anita property, became the superintendent. The partnership's sheep multiplied rapidly. Wool prices were increased by the Civil War, and the vast profits made by the alliance enabled them to buy enormous acreage of land at prices depressed by the great drought in the 1860s, when most of the large bankrupted ranchos were forced to sell property.

In the Gaviota Land, after José Francisco Ortega's death, his lands were inherited by his grandson Antonio Maria Ortega (child of José Maria Ortega) and daughter-in-law Magdalena Cota Ortega (wife of his son José Francisco Maria Ortega). On April 25, 1854, an agreement gave the west half of the ranch (Cojo to Gaviota) to Magdalena, while Antonio Maria received the eastern half of the Ortega grant, which encompassed most of Gaviota. When Magdalena died on October 12, 1862, her properties in the Hollister area were divided between four of her children—her son, José Vicente Estefano Ortega and her daughters Dolores (Raymundo Carrillo), Manuela (Guillermo Carrillo), and Refugio (Luis Carrillo).

The Gaviota parcel was the first portion of the Nuestra Señora del Refugio grant to be sold outside the family, and the drought contributed to its transfer and the controversial lawsuits which resulted. The parcel first went to Antonio Maria's son, José Manuel Ortega (whose wife was Maria Josepa Lugo), and was then sold to Andrea Cota Ortega Olivera, their niece, on January 11, 1858, for $2,500. Andrea and her husband, Mariano, signed a promissory note on that date for $987.50, which was satisfied December 23, 1859, but it appeared that the Oliveras had to borrow $800 from John Temple (husband of Andrea's sister Rafaela) to do so. When they were not able to repay the note, Temple received a foreclosure judgment on December 22, 1865; but five days before, the Oliveras had sold the Gaviota Rancho to Andrea's other sister, Clara Cota Lobero, and her husband, José, for $2,000, which caused the confusion. The Loberos also purchased José Vicente Estefan's Santa Anita Rancho for $1,500, and Thomas Dibblee bought them both for $4,000 in April 1866.

The foreclosure and previous sale resulted in conflicting claims of ownership for several years. The Oliveras had 500 head of cattle before the drought and also pastured 200 head belonging to the firm of Domingo Abadia & Brothers. Gaviota Rancho was mortgaged for their faithful performance. William Abadia had a judgment in April 1864 against the firm, which required public auction of the Gaviota cattle, and this occurred at the Olivera adobe. Abadia purchased the animals for $200, but they were all dead from the drought. Temple had also foreclosed on the Gaviota Rancho, which was auctioned at the Santa Barbara courthouse on February 6, 1866, and he was the high bidder at $1,221.45. Abadia paid him the amount of the lien and tried to get possession but was not successful, and

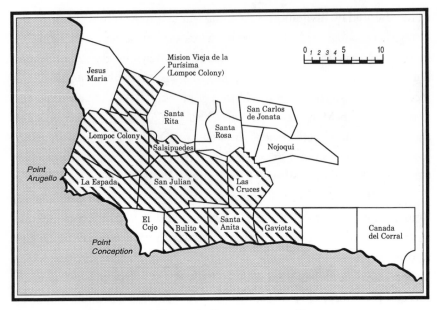

HOLLISTER-DIBBLEE PARTNERSHIP RANCHES

Thomas Dibblee retained the land.

Dolores's parcel was sold in December 1865 to Thomas Sprague for $1,000. Thomas Dibblee purchased it in August 1866. Manuela's land went to Thomas Dibblee for $1,500 in October 1866. Refugio's property was purchased by Thomas Sprague for $1,300 in June 1865, and Thomas Dibblee acquired this too in August 1866. It is estimated that nearly three fourths of the original Nuestra Señora del Refugio grant of the Ortegas had been purchased by Thomas Dibblee by 1866. One-third interests were deeded to his brother, Albert, and to William Hollister as part of their partnership.

The alliance purchases eventually included the contiguous acres of Nuestra Señora del Refugio, San Julian, Las Cruces, Lompoc, Mission Vieja, and Salsipuedes ranchos—massive acreage. Their combined holdings added up to well over 125,000 acres, with 20 miles or more of ocean frontage, and the Gaviota Land was part of the vast Hollister and Dibblee empire. Hollister lived in Santa Barbara and was involved financially with many projects there, while management of the large partnership's empire was from the San Julian headquarters.

Rancho San Julian adobe.

Rancho San Julian. The headquarters rancho had been known as a "kitchen" ranch (Rancho Nacional), as it provided meat for the Santa Barbara Presidio and also a great deal of tallow and leather. The land was granted in 1837 to Don José de la Guerra, former presidio comandante, in lieu of $12,000 in back pay. The drought of 1863-1864 caused severe financial problems, and the land was mortgaged to Gaspar Orena. The Hollister-Dibblee partnership purchased the property in 1867. Thomas Dibblee later married Francisca de la Guerra, daughter of Don José de la Guerra's son, Pablo.

The center section and left wing of the headquarters adobe at Rancho San Julian were built by the De la Guerras. Thomas Dibblee added the right wing in 1878. Supplies arrived at the Gaviota wharf to be transported to the ranch by ox-drawn wagons. The ranch had its own meat and vegetables, and for a long time food was prepared by the different Chinese cooks. Buildings and homes for the men were later constructed, and a one-room school for twenty to twenty-five local children came into existence around 1910. It had a fireplace and a large, unique back that opened up and brought the outdoors inside. The old San Julian Road passed right next to the school. In later years, the ranch had six silos and a dairy. The dairy was originally designed for the use of the ranch families, but it later became a large grade-A dairy that handled over seventy-five cows.

San Julian School.

The Sheep Domain. The vast acres of the partnership empire provided grazing for thousands of merino sheep, which were constantly herded by shepherds. The animals were usually kept in flocks of several thousand, and there were many camps, each located close to water and containing a one-room hut with a table, cupboard, wood stove, chair, and bed. An out-house and corral were also part of the small complex. The corral was frequently made from tree branches, sticks, and brush. These were convenient, lasted for years, and the wild animals could not get through them as easily as other enclosures.

Herders usually had at least one dog to be alert for strange sounds or intruders. Supplies from headquarters were sent regularly on pack animals. The shepherds could also kill sheep for their needs. Meat was made into jerky, and scraps fed the dogs. Sometimes in summer, the herder might move with his flock and live under the trees. At shearing time, each herder brought his flock to headquarters, where a large wool barn, three holding corrals, pens, platform, and a dip were available. Additional men were hired, some of whom came from the Caire family at the completion of their shearing on Santa Cruz Island. About 1,500 sheep were brought into the corrals at a time, and about 150 went to the platform and three pens; the other animals remained in fenced pastures.

Bleating filled the air as shearing took place. It usually took ten to twenty minutes to shear each animal, and a good worker could clip forty animals a day. Smaller sections of wool from the face, legs, and breast were picked up separately, but the wool from the back, sides, and loins usually came off in one piece. The wool went into a chute to the baler, where it was bundled into 400-pound bales for storage in the barn. It took weeks before all the flocks were shorn. The spring clipping was considered better than the fall, because foxtails and other grass seeds had not proliferated enough to cause problems in the wool. Workers received a token for each sheep shorn, and these were later exchanged for money, with each token worth about fifteen cents in 1880. These were made at Rancho San Julian with the partnership brand in the center—a "D" with a "+" in the middle.

After shearing, sheep went through a gate to slide into a warm bath of water mixed with such ingredients as tobacco juice, sulfur, and lime for the control of scabs and ticks. A large boiler under the dip heated the water. The ramp going out was cleated to enable the animals to climb out, and they were then returned to the grazing hills so they would not get mixed up with others. Lambs were weaned at this time, and the animals that were ready for shipment to San Francisco (generally the wethers or older ewes) were separated to be sent to Gaviota. Before the wharf was built, the sheep were sent out to ships in tenders or had to swim out while boats guided them, but their wool got soggy and wet.

Cattle Drives. There was greater sheep competition in later years, and as wool prices declined, cattle again became the mainstay of ranches, not for the hides and tallow, but for meat. Annual spring roundups were extensive operations, involving separating, vaccinating, and branding the animals. The calves particularly needed to be vaccinated before they got too old and the grass was too high, or "black leg," a disease like anthrax, would be a threat.

In earlier days, riders had herded the animals to a "holding ground" where they were contained by other vaqueros. Corrals to contain the animals were later built in different ranch areas. The roping of animals was usually done by two or three men. The head was caught first, then the feet were looped, and the animal was "heeled" and stretched out. It was put on

Roundup at Rancho San Julian.

A cattle drive going through Las Cruces to Gaviota.

its side while two horses backed up just enough to keep ropes taut. Ear-marks were made on the right ear with a clipper, and a "jaw brand" was put on heifers to identify age. The males were altered, and budding horns were removed to prevent bruising and damage before shipment to market along with the barren cows. The cattle to be sold for beef were often driven first to headquarters for the consummation of the sale before shipment. They

82

A cattle drive going from Rancho San Julian to Gaviota.

were put into the corral overnight without feed, then weighed. If they had eaten, their weight was discounted appropriately.

The long drives to the Gaviota wharf were made in the late spring or early summer, and it was then generally dry and dusty. There were often wide distances between straggling cattle, and interspersed riders were needed to propel the herd along. From the headquarters they followed the road as far as La Golondrina, about three miles away, then trudged up over the hills. The animals drank a great deal of water from a good spring about halfway up. At the top of the ridge was a spectacular view of the Gaviota area, which included the ocean and coast for miles. The cattle then ran rapidly down the other side of the hill to Las Cruces, where they remained in corrals during lunchtime. After crossing over the Gaviota Creek, the drive continued through the pass and on to the wharf, where the animals were loaded onto ships. (After the Pacific Coast Railway was built to Guadalupe, cattle were sometimes driven there, about thirty miles.)

When early automobiles were on the road, a rider waving a red bandana preceded the herd to warn approaching motorists. Drivers were generally able to get by in a few minutes, but for those in a hurry, a rider went through the herd to make passage for the vehicle. Sometimes animals go-

The ship Santa Cruz *at the Gaviota wharf, circa 1888.*

ing in the same direction as a car tried to run ahead of it. Both cattle and automobiles shared U.S. 101 until the 1920s, and the Highway Patrol helped decrease accidents; but as the flood of automobiles increased, the long drives through the Gaviota Pass had to be terminated.

The Wharf and Shipping
Before the Gaviota wharf was built at Port Orford, steamer mail could sometimes be left on the beach for pickup by anyone going into town, and passengers had to be carried to land. Lumber was floated in on tides, and schooners from the mills of Santa Cruz and other locations had to anchor

Gaviota Canyon circa 1875, with the presumed Burke adobe in the fore-ground. Note the ship at anchor in the distance.

in deep water to dump their loads of up to 40,000 board feet at once. It had to be quickly retrieved from the beach or the sea would reclaim it. Cattle had to swim to shore. Animals from the Channel Islands were brought as close as possible to Gaviota (about 400 yards) before being driven overboard. (Once, a confused cow arrived on shore but not through her own efforts. She swam in the wrong direction—out to sea— and it was the tide that returned her to the beach.)

The wharf franchise was issued to Hollister and the Dibblees in 1875 and 1895. It was considered an important artery in the county. The structure was initially built as the outlet for the vast partnership empire to handle all the wool, cattle, and grain produced on their ranches. The wool was sent to San Francisco, the chief market on the west coast, and then on to Boston, the prominent wool-manufacturing center. For years, the Gaviota wharf also handled the produce from Santa Ynez, Lompoc, and surrounding areas.

Miguel Burke was one wharf manager. He had a store and an inn at the mouth of Gaviota Canyon, and Henry McNealy was in charge later. The wharf, which extended at least one thousand feet into the water, had a depth of twenty-five feet, and giant steamers stopped there for passengers and freight. Although strong winds would occasionally come down

85

Gaviota Canyon, the wharf was considered a "safe landing," and it was a preferred port of entry for many people coming to the area. There was a warehouse for storage on the land side of the wharf and a small building with a wood stove on the ocean end, where many individuals huddled by grain sacks to wait for morning transportation.

It has been said the founding of Lompoc resulted from a meeting at Gaviota. (Lompoc is said to mean "little lakes," and the Spanish called it Lompoco.) William Broughton, a lawyer and newspaperman from Santa Cruz, came on a lumber vessel to Gaviota. There he met George Long, superintendent for the Hollister-Dibblee empire, who took Broughton for a ride through the country. Feeling that Lompoc would be a good location for a temperance colony, Broughton returned to Santa Cruz to make arrangements. It took several years to make plans and get stockholders, but finally an auction was scheduled for November 9, 1874. The land was advertised October 31 in the Santa Cruz *Sentinel*, and special arrangements with the Goodall, Nelson, and Perkins Steamship Company's vessels were made for travel from San Francisco to Gaviota on November 3. The steamer *Senator* of the Pacific Mail Steamship Company also left on November, to stop first at Santa Cruz to board additional passengers for Gaviota. Travelers from both ships were to be met at Gaviota and transported to Lompoc.

The Lompoc community twice built its own thousand-foot wharf at Lompoc Landing, but severe storms along the coast destroyed both wharves. The Gaviota wharf, therefore, remained the nearest port of entry for Lompoc. Gaviota Pass was then only wide enough for one wagon, and the road from Lompoc was private and required the opening and closing of many gates. Parts of the road were really only cow paths, and rain often made the trip very difficult. Drivers had to be careful not to meet an oncoming stage or another wagon on the narrow road and stopped at wide spots to listen for sounds before continuing.

Records indicate that the lumber for the old Lompoc Methodist Church arrived at Gaviota. Another shipment to arrive at Gaviota was lumber and 20,000 shingles for the Presbyterian Church in Ballard. The latter had been shipped from Oregon and took two days to haul by wagon through Gaviota Pass. A load of lumber for the hotel being built by a

A grain wagon underway from Lompoc to Gaviota.

Santa Ynez land syndicate and wood for Rufus Buell's unique forty-mile, five-board redwood fence also arrived at the Gaviota wharf.

Outlet for the Santa Ynez Valley. The Gaviota wharf was the outlet for the entire Santa Ynez Valley, where grain was the main harvest, and thirty to fifty farmers hauled heavy sacks to the wharf each week. They had to travel in big wagons over streams and steep, narrow, rocky roads. The route went by the Santa Inés Mission, over the Nojoqui Grade, down to Las Cruces, and on through the Gaviota Pass. The trip took one day each way, and the road crisscrossed Gaviota Creek many times. Often lumber, produce, and passengers were transported back to the Santa Ynez Valley. Drivers usually stopped to spend the night at Las Cruces before their return trip the next morning to make preparations for another wharf trip.

There was a great deal of competition between teamsters to get to the wharf ahead of others and to avoid the long lines, and consequently they sometimes sabotaged each other. One of their many tricks was to detain the rig behind them by pouring water on the banks of a stream after crossing it. The next reinsman would have to fight to get his heavy carriage out of the mud, and a third teamster probably had to help him, or *he* wouldn't be able to get across either. This could have happened more than once per trip, for there were fourteen creek crossings. It is said that one driver dragged a dead tree across the road in order to make a more defiant block-ade for those who followed.

After the produce sacks were unloaded, most drivers unhitched their lead horses in order to navigate the turn around the warehouse. One man made it with a six-horse team, but another driver's wagon tilted on the edge, the harness broke, and the front animals fell over the side, pulling the others in with them. They did reach shore, however.

Chickens were often found along the road, gobbling grain that had spilled from the bouncing wagons, and an experienced driver could crack a long whip adroitly across the back of a hen's neck as he continued on down the road without stopping. The following driver picked up the fowl for dinner.

Steamship Companies and Ships. Channel steamship service was furnished by Pacific Mail Steamship Company in 1865. In 1867, Pacific Mail merged with Goodall, Nelson, and Perkins, and this became the Pacific Coast Steamship Company, with about twenty-four ports along the California coast. A controlling interest was sold to the Oregon Improvement Company in 1881, and the Pacific Coast Company consequently became the successor. Their Narrow Gauge Route included San Francisco, Santa Cruz, Monterey, San Simeon, Cayucos, Port Harford (San Luis Obispo), Lompoc, Gaviota (Port Orford), Santa Barbara, San Buenaventura, Hueneme, San Pedro, and Newport Landing.

Some of the ships docking at the Gaviota wharf were the *Orizaba, Los Angeles, Eureka, Queen of the Pacific, Ancon, Coos Bay,* and *Santa Rosa.* Going south in August 1887, the *Los Angeles* arrived at Gaviota on the 8th, 16th, and 24th. The *Eureka* arrived the 4th, 12th, 20th, and 28th. Going north, the *Los Angeles* arrived on August 3rd, 11th, 19th, and 27th, and the *Eureka* the 7th, 15th, 23rd, and 31st.

One of the most popular and favored ships docking at Gaviota was the *Santa Rosa,* the largest of the Pacific Coast Steamship Company's fleet. It stopped on both north- and south-bound trips, and traveled the route for twenty-five years. Sadly, this respected steamer ended its voyages July 7, 1911, when it ran aground at low tide near the mouth of Honda Creek north of Point Arguello. A loud shrill arose from the wounded vessel,

The Santa Rosa *ran aground and broke up on the rocks near Honda.*

hunks of wood flew all over, and the vessel's "back" was broken as it split in half. The first life-raft, carrying a number of women and children, turned over in the surf, but eventually all 200 passengers reached shore, although their belongings were left behind. The ship was declared a total loss, and by the end of the next month, the hulk was half-sunk in the sand.

Fire damaged the wharf in 1885, but it was promptly repaired. A permit was granted in 1895 to do some rebuilding and enlarging, but when the railroad was completed, the siding and depot at Gaviota handled the shipments that once went from the wharf. The fast steel rails replaced the slow ocean vessels. The wharf was purchased by the Pacific Coast Steamship Company in 1888, and the property was later sold to the Honolulu Oil Company. During a terrific storm, the outer edge of the wharf and the warehouse broke off and floated out to sea. A great deal of the main structure had disappeared before 1912, and pilings continued to go out through the 1930s. One lone set of pilings, however, was still visible in 1939. A few "stubs" can still be seen off the beach at very low tide. An historic era in the Gaviota Land had ended.

Partnership Dissolution and Dispositions

The Hollister-Dibblee partnership continued in the operation of the wharf, but was severed otherwise by mutual agreement in the early 1880s. Hollister had been involved in costly law suits over his home in Santa Barbara, and his health was not good. It was thought best to divide the land and livestock. The La Purísima and Mission Vieja ranches had already been sold in 1874 for $500,000 to establish the Lompoc Colony. Other lands, the La Espada and El Cojo ranches, went to the Sudden and Bixby families. At the dissolution of the partnership, the Dibblees owed Hollister $50,000, and land was mortgaged in order to clear this debt. The Dibblees originally had the San Julian and Gaviota coastal area to Arroyo Hondo, but Hollister desired to trade Jalama for the Gaviota coastal acreage. Consequently, the Dibblees had over 48,000 acres of Rancho San Julian and Jalama. Hollister held title to the Salsipuedes, Las Cruces, Santa Anita, and Gaviota areas. (Hollister also had the Winchester area, which was not part of the partnership acreage.)

Thomas and Albert divided their lands around 1891. They both died in 1895. Albert's family inherited Jalama, and Thomas's descendants received the 25,000 acres of San Julian. A great deal of Jalama was sold between 1910 and 1920, but about 14,000 (not all contiguous) acres of Rancho San Julian still remain in the Dibblee family. Thomas Dibblee's will decreed that when the youngest of his five children reached thirty-five years of age, a drawing of sections would be held among his widow and children. Seven parcels were divided in 1918, and the house and surrounding 4,000 acres were to be held by the family in an undivided interest, in trust for the following generation. The fate of the Hollister Ranch forms a later chapter of our story.

CHAPTER 7

The Railroad Gap

Pacific Coast Railway

The railroads superseded the old wharf for transportation. The first rails in the area were the 103 miles of the narrow gauge "iron pony," which originated at Port Harford in Avila Bay. When these tracks reached Los Olivos, they became competition for the Gaviota wharf.

John Harford and a group of San Luis Obispo merchants formed the People's Wharf Company around 1868, and an 1,800-foot wharf was built for a narrow gauge, horse-drawn railroad, which went from the wharf to a warehouse onshore. The enterprise became known as the San Luis Obispo Railway in 1873, when tracks reached that city. Rails for steam-powered engines were extended to Central City (Santa Maria) and Los Alamos in 1882. The railway merged to become the Pacific Coast Railway, incorporated April 18, 1882 under the Oregon Improvement Company, and the enterprise reached Los Olivos, but that remained the end of the line.

The Pacific Coast Company purchased the property of the Oregon Improvement Company in 1897 and controlled both the steamship and railroad lines. Use of the little narrow-gauge railroad started to dwindle as competition grew from the "iron horse," the Southern Pacific, and trucking later became another competitive form of transportation. Most of the narrow gauge was abandoned between 1937 and 1940, and there is almost no trace left of the little railroad.

The Southern Pacific Railroad and the "Gap"

Before the coastal rail route was completed, Gaviota was part of the well-

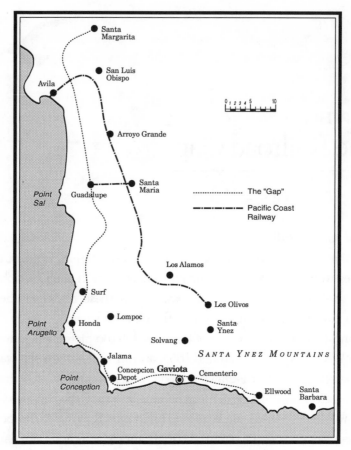

THE SOUTHERN PACIFIC RAILROAD GAP

known "gap" that existed for many years. The Southern Pacific had inland tracks down the San Joaquin Valley and was constructing a coast route from Los Angeles to San Francisco. In 1873, tracks were laid at Soledad, about 144 miles south of San Francisco, and the loading chutes at this terminus were the destination for cattle drives for a while. Herds were driven from as far south as San Diego, and Gaviota Pass was the preferred route for those going through the Santa Ynez and Los Alamos valleys on their way to Soledad. Flocks contained up to 2,000 animals, and the cattle were allowed to cross over private land if they were kept moving at a reasonable rate, but local animals often joined the herd, and ranch representatives sometimes had to go to Soledad to retrieve their strays.

In the spring of 1886, the Southern Pacific began construction north of Los Angeles at Saugus, and rails came to the coast—Santa Paula in January 1887, Ventura in May, and Santa Barbara in August. Everyone felt that through transportation was going to be available between San Francisco and Los Angeles. The rails, however, only crawled a few more miles to Ellwood and didn't go any further for years. That became one end of the gap. In the north, the Southern Pacific reached King City by July 1886, Paso Robles in October, Templeton in November, and Santa Margarita in January 1887. That was the other end of the 123-mile gap, which was to last for a long fourteen years.

Through rail transportation was desperately needed. Stages had to be taken from Santa Margarita to Santa Barbara to make rail connections inland for Saugus in order to go south. To venture north from Santa Barbara, travelers took the stage to Los Olivos, stayed the night, and boarded the narrow gauge to San Luis Obispo, where they took another stage to Santa Margarita for rail transportation to San Francisco.

Part of the reason for the gap was an economic depression. The bottom had dropped out of the economy, and several railroads had already gone bankrupt. Large amounts of funds were necessary to span the gap; there were numerous grades along this section which required large fills, tunnels, or long trestles. At one time, it was thought that no fewer than twenty-seven spans would be required. Routes had to be surveyed, and rights of way obtained.

One of the more important decisions was what route to take through the Gaviota Land. One possible route turned inland over Gaviota Pass. It was first thought that this would be the course chosen and that the rails would make the same turn at Gaviota as the road. The Dibblees had hoped that such a line would extend from the wharf to Rancho San Julian and on into Lompoc, and it is said that they even offered free right of way and a cash incentive. But a survey of the Gaviota Pass route was made in August 1886 by Joseph Hood, and another was done in September 1887 by W.B. Story, and these surveys found that too many tunnels and bridges would be needed on the Gaviota Pass route, so it was rejected.

The other, longer route went along the coast and around Point Conception, but it didn't have the heavy grades of the pass route. The first survey of this course created a crooked and winding railroad but one that required few cuts and fills. The route that was finally adopted went as straight as possible but did require extensive filling, numerous viaducts, and several tunnels.

When work began on the gap, thousands of workmen and many contractors participated. Support people included bookkeepers, timekeepers, cooks, and blacksmiths. Construction on the rails to Santa Barbara had been performed mainly by Chinese, but now mostly Caucasians were hired. Progress was slow, as the work had to be done mostly by men and mules. Rains, labor shortages, and threatened lawsuits also delayed progress. Numerous steel bridges required additional time, as abutments had to be built before piers could be sunk into the earth, many thirty or forty feet deep. Numerous camps formed clusters of white tents with corrals for the hundreds of animals, and temporary "stores" sold miscellaneous

Tents housing railroad construction workers were surrounded with corrals for draft animals.

goods at lofty prices. Workers were charged $5.25 a week for lodging with meals. Many teams of animals were brought in, but $10 a month was also paid for good local animals, and contractors provided feed, shoeing, and animal care.

The contractors encountered many problems. The camps attracted saloons, gambling, and prostitution. They were noisy at night, and the men were often "under the weather" the next day. There were three saloons in Las Cruces, and when one worker displayed a roll of bills in one of them, he was killed shortly after leaving. McMurtrie & Stone tried to alleviate some of the difficulties by paying men in scrip redeemable at company stores. There was also a shortage of labor; pay was not high, work was strenuous, and accidents did happen. Some injuries were from blasting, and one worker fell from a viaduct.

Work on the gap started from the north, and heavy construction was necessary in the mountains over Cuesta Grade. Six tunnels and the famous horseshoe curve were built between Santa Margarita and San Luis Obispo, and service from San Francisco became available in May 1894. Travelers from the Gaviota and Santa Barbara areas still had to take the stage to Los Olivos before they could board the narrow gauge for San Luis Obispo to connect with the Southern Pacific, but they were spared the stage trip to Santa Margarita.

The rails reached Guadalupe in August 1895 and Surf in August 1896, but they were still fifty-six miles from the dormant steel at Ellwood. The newly created town of Bridgeport sprouted up near Surf but ceased to exist a short time later. The branch line to Lompoc, about eleven miles inland, was constructed in 1899, allowing trains from San Francisco to arrive there daily, and Lompoc became the stage terminus for transportation to San Francisco by rail.

Between Surf and Ellwood, tracks had to be laid on the cliffs along the coast. Construction was difficult, and a great deal of work was necessary, including several tunnels, many fills, and steel viaducts. Depots were to be established at Goleta, Naples, Gaviota, Point Conception (the station's name was spelled Concepcion), Sudden, and Surf. It was thought that Naples and Gaviota would probably be water stops, while the others would be flag stops.

The small town of Bridgeport during construction on the railroad gap.

Construction on the railroad gap nears Gaviota.

Coming down the coast from Surf, the Honda viaduct was constructed in December 1898. The next trestle was at Jalama. There was also an 811-foot tunnel in this section, built by Carney, Roy & Higbeer, but it was demolished in the 1950s. The railroad turned at the "heel of the California foot," Point Conception, and around the corner a large fill at Cojo was completed about March, thought to be the largest on the Southern Pacific lines—270,000 cubic yards—and built by Charles Erickson.

The railroad was now on the "home stretch" toward Gaviota, but a great deal of work remained to be done to complete this last link. Eight trestles had to be constructed in a little more than eighteen miles. In October 1889, it was reported that one thousand men and seventeen camps were in the vicinity. The railroad acquired a sixty-foot right of way along Hollister's twenty-mile stretch of coast and would build sidings at San Augustine and Drake, which would also have a depot and section house. The Hollister family was also to obtain free lifetime rail travel. A viaduct across Santa Anita Canyon was also part of the agreement, but a large and controversial fill of 1,500-2,000 cubic feet was put there instead; this obstructed the ocean view, and so the family home was moved two miles westward to El Bulito Canyon.

At one place along the route there was a landslide. Part of the roadbed slipped toward the ocean, and seawalls had to be constructed. At other locations, it was necessary to move the track further inland. At one time, it is thought, a temporary wharf near Gaviota was considered for delivery of materials by steamer. Lumber was floated to shore in some places, but most of the supplies arrived as close as possible by rail.

Continuing toward Gaviota, a large cut of about 83,000 cubic yards had to be made in the hill between Gato and San Augustine canyons. A 715-foot tunnel, built by E.J. Carney, was put in between Drake and Sacate (taken out around 1943). By the end of May 1899, construction trains were coming up to the viaduct at Alegria, only about four miles from Gaviota. The next overpass was built at Agua Caliente. (These two trestles were later known as trestle #2 and trestle #1 by those in the Gaviota Land.) Finally the longest trestle of the gap was erected in November 1900 at Gaviota. The trestle was 811 feet long and 80 feet high, and a siding and a depot were provided at its east end. The rails waited

Trestle #1 (above) and #2 (below).

there for other steel from the south to join them; this was to be the last section of the gap.

Construction finally started at Ellwood in March 1899, and contractor P.J. McCormick had around 125 men engaged with 90 teams. Between Ellwood and Naples three massive fills were required, and viaducts were necessary at Dos Pueblos, El Capitan, Refugio, Arroyo Hondo, and Cementerio. It took over a year to construct only four miles of track, but progress was being made. Soon the tracks were only 750 feet apart, and around the end of December 1900, the last rail was laid, and the final spike was driven at Gaviota (Cementerio). The gap was now part of the history

Trestle construction near Gaviota.

Close-up of trestle at Gaviota.

The first train to reach Santa Barbara after the gap was closed.

of the Gaviota Land.

The railroad was not in operation quite yet, however, for other work still remained to be done, including the completion of some station buildings and track ballasting. The Coast Line was finally opened on Sunday, March 31, 1901, and the first scheduled train was the No. 1 *Coast Line Limited*. The same day the railroad opened, the stagecoaches made their last trip (except for the run to Gaviota from the Los Olivos area), and the mail franchise was transferred to the rails.

During the *Coast Line's* first few months, there were three serious derailments between Santa Barbara and Gaviota. The rails could not handle the large volume of traffic and the heavy trains that were using them. The track had to be re-laid using stronger steel, and the line remained closed for repairs until December, when these improvements put Gaviota on the main line of the transcontinental railroad system. Travelers went from Gaviota to Santa Barbara for $1.35, and the *Lark* and *Daylight* trains chugged up and down the coast for years. One of the modern passenger trains crossing the Gaviota trestle in May 1971 was run by Amtrak, providing coastal service from Seattle to San Diego.

The bridges along the gap still stand. Girders have been reinforced or replaced, and additional bents have been placed on some of them. Piers

An Amtrak train crosses the Gaviota trestle.

have been added or modified, and most of the original open decks have been ballasted, but they are still the original structures. The viaduct at Gaviota is dated 1898, erected November 1900. Additional intermediate bents were placed there in 1935, and girders, bents, and bracing were reinforced. It was converted to a ballasted deck in 1952.

The Gaviota Depot

Large section gangs were needed to maintain the long sections of track, and many lived in small houses not far from the Gaviota depot. The railroad also had sleeping cars, and the "restaurant" was a dining car that was kept stocked by passing trains. The men were transported back and forth to work by rail.

The railroad was now the prime transportation medium for cattle shipments; the station at Gaviota took precedence over the narrow gauge at Los Olivos and the transfer to the Southern Pacific at San Luis Obispo. Through rail transportation was available, and large cattle drives were made to the Gaviota depot and corrals, located close to the cliffs across from the old Gaviota Store.

The two-story depot was typical of others. The agent lived upstairs, and an office and a waiting room with an iron stove and benches for the passengers were downstairs. The agent was also the telegrapher, transmitting by Morse code. He made communication directly with passing trains by putting information into a hoop which was grabbed by the engineer as the train passed. Return data for him was thrown out on the ground.

The cattle at the depot were loaded into cars at the siding, and each car held approximately forty animals. The local train was supposed to stop for the full cars; if it did not, the next freight train would have to be flagged. At least one ranch representative made sure the cattle were picked up and arrived at their destination. The livestock could die if the cars they were in were sidetracked en route, but they generally reached market the next day. If the animals were in the cars too long, however, they would have to be unloaded and fed. After reaching the stockyards, they were auctioned off or delivered to the buyer who had already purchased them at the ranches.

Sometimes cattle also arrived at the depot. In February 1926, it was reported that one thousand head had been shipped in thirty-five cars to Gaviota to be herded over Alisal Road to the San Marcos Ranch.

The cattle drives to the depot probably ended in the 1930s, when trucks came directly to the ranches to pick up animals. The station at Gaviota is no longer in existence. It was removed in the 1960s, and those cattle drives are now things of the past.

Other Railroad Information

Hollister Ranch had numerous fires because of the railroad. Crews threw sand into the engine's flue to clean it out, and this generated sparks which set fire to hillside brush. Wet sacks were sometimes used to try to smother the sparks, but in 1940 a spark started a massive blaze that charred everything up to the top of the ridge, including the fence.

A few other incidents were connected with the railroad. President William McKinley traveled over the rails in May 1901, and President Theodore Roosevelt crossed the Gaviota trestle in the same month two years later, stopping at Surf to speak. Nikita Khrushchev, premier of the USSR, visited the United States in September 1959, and armed guards were on the Gaviota trestle; additional guards rode on top of the train.

Another train that passed over Gaviota's rails came to disaster around Point Conception in May 1907. Most of the passengers were from a

Theodore Roosevelt speaking at Surf after crossing the trestle at Gaviota.

Shriners' convention in Los Angeles. The locomotive suddenly jumped off the rails at Honda and capsized into a ditch. The following cars skidded along the tracks, bent, and crashed into and over each other. Steam escaping from ruptured pipes inside the diner killed many passengers. The cause of the accident is not known.

Two girls fell from the Gaviota trestle in 1910. They were walking over the narrow track when a train suddenly appeared behind them, and afraid of being crushed, they hung over the side as long as possible. Esther Smith was killed. Her companion lived, but her name is not known. The engineer reported that he had been afraid to apply the brakes for fear of breaking or damaging the trestle.

A serious railroad accident occurred near Gaviota in 1917, when seven freight cars tumbled into the ditch; four turned over. Although it required many hours to clear the track, no one was injured. A broken draw bar was thought to be the cause.

The rails changed lifestyles. No longer did stagecoaches and wagons travel to the Gaviota wharf where the large steamers blew their whistles and docked. Around the turn of the century in the Gaviota Land, one era ended as another began.

Gaviota Pass Road before the automobile age.

CHAPTER 8

Roads and Highways

The Gaviota Pass County Road

Railroads made vast changes in transportation, but automobiles and highways did also. In early years, the original path of El Camino Real followed
the coast along the same route traveled by Portolá, but the establishment
of the La Purísima (1787) and Santa Inés (1804) missions resulted in
travel turning inland. There were three passes through the Santa Ynez
Mountains, but wandering over them was very difficult. It was said that
travelers meandered over a multitude of mountains to avoid crossing one.
Gaviota Pass was the lowest in elevation, 950 feet (with Refugio Pass at
2,250 feet, and San Marcos Pass at 2,225 feet).

Initially, San Marcos Pass was just an Indian trail, and Refugio Pass
was a route from the Ortega Rancho to the Santa Inés Mission. Gaviota
Pass was the only true mountain pass, but it was very narrow and was
sometimes blocked by boulders that rolled down the steep cliffs; landslides
were always a danger. Wagons had not been able to get through until
1854, when pioneers chiseled at the cliffs for days to make a large enough
opening; before that, vehicles had to be transferred through in pieces.
Colonel Hollister tore down his sister's wagon to get it beyond this slender
mountain passageway.

The first county road through Gaviota Pass was built in 1861, primarily for stages. Dynamite had to be used to widen the small crevice at the
pass, and a wooden bridge was constructed over the creek. The massive
Los Angeles and Santa Barbara counties were contiguous then, and they
cooperated to gain a reliable thoroughfare between them. Los Angeles

105

The county road allowed the change from wagons to automobiles.

106

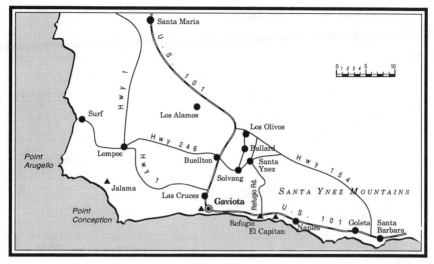

HIGHWAYS LINKING GAVIOTA AND SURROUNDING TOWNS

County allocated $2,000 for their portion of a "good" road to the county line; Santa Barbara County held a special bond election on May 21, 1859, to raise $15,000 for their share, and the state legislature appropriated another $15,000 for the project. T. Wallace More, a large landholder, was awarded the contract for $15,000, but he did not meet his commitments. Bridges weren't built, fills were rejected, and unprecedented rain required time extensions. Suit was brought against him for reneging on the agreement, and the contract was given to James Thompson, a Los Angeles engineer.

The road was a big improvement, but repair work was necessary in 1881. Its roughness was bad, but narrowness was an even greater hazard. Wagons could not get by each other in many places, serpentine curves obstructed visibility, and weather wiped out some areas. At least one section was on record as being impassable in November 1885 because of mud and debris from heavy rains.

Highway Modifications

Improvements resulted when the State Division of Highways took over the road around 1915. The county provided maintenance for bypasses and bridges; the state graveled unpaved sections. This was thought to provide

107

a "splendid" highway from Santa Barbara through the Gaviota Pass to Santa Maria and areas north. The route was also altered. The communities inland from the Gaviota Land had hoped that the railroad would reach them. It did not. They also hoped that the main highway, when it developed, would follow the old stagecoach route, which had gone from Gaviota through Nojoqui, Ballard, Los Olivos, and Santa Maria before heading north. It did not. The chosen course went through Gaviota but bypassed the others, going through the new town of Buellton to Santa Maria. This highway change stunted the growth of the other communities, but it gave "birth" to Buellton (originally Servicetown, USA). The route became the heavily traveled U.S. Highway 101.

During these road modifications, about seventy-five men and teams worked between Las Cruces and Gaviota Pass, where a steel suspension bridge was built in place of the wooden span. James Donahue was the local contractor, and his work served until 1931, when the increase in traffic demanded major reconstruction of the three and one-half miles of highway through the gorge. The lanes were straightened, repaved, and widened. The winding and curling Gaviota Creek was a problem. In a three-mile distance, it was estimated that nineteen structures were necessary to put a bridge over each crossing. To avoid this, major changes were made to the creek, and retaining walls helped guard the roadbeds. The new concourse had a twenty-foot concrete surface with a nine-foot gravel shoulder on each side. An expenditure of $275,000 was allocated—a costly figure per mile at that time—$40,000 to $50,000 of which went toward preserving the natural beauty of Gaviota Pass.

A principal part of the construction was a new 190-foot reinforced concrete overpass, which replaced the old steel suspension bridge. (The old bridge was subsequently moved by horses and placed over a Hollister ravine; it was later scrapped. Relocation was said to have cost $6,000.) The new structure was built at an angle that permitted standard highway width without having to blast the pass. Two very dangerous curves, which had been the location of many accidents, were eliminated, and traffic was one-way-only in many places until the work was completed in October 1931.

At first it was declared that the overhanging rock that dominated the

Steel suspension bridge through Gaviota Pass.

A concrete overpass replaced the steel suspension bridge.

west side of Gaviota Pass was a danger to highway traffic and would have to be removed. This large piece of granite resembled the head of an Indian and was considered to be a prominent part of the fissure, a "spirit guardian." After numerous protests, plans were changed. Ladders were built to allow access up the steep cliffs in order to make some safety modifications, but most of the original rock was retained. It remains the "sentinel" of the pass.

Although the ladders were only visible from certain areas, they were noticed in later years, and there was speculation over their origin. Some people thought pirates or bandits had used them for burying loot in the inaccessible cliff caves. Another theory was that they were used to gather honey from wild bees. Some felt that Indians had been responsible for them, but the milled lumber of which they were built spoiled this theory. The true reason for their existence was revealed when a construction worker remembered their use during road work; they had just been abandoned on the cliffs when they were no longer needed.

Another major improvement was made in 1934, when nearly five miles of the old inadequate road between Gaviota and Arroyo Hondo were replaced, widened, and straightened by the Weymouth-Crowell Company of Los Angeles. The new section of highway replaced innumer-

Two-way traffic shared the road before the Gaviota tunnel was built.

able curves; forty-one were reduced to ten. A grade line was adopted to retain the view of the ocean as much as possible, and soil was brought in for a concrete pavement base, as native ground was not considered suitable. The cost of about $65,000 per mile was underwritten and governed by the National Industrial Recovery Act.

Construction work from Las Cruces to near Buellton was done in 1935. That section contained forty-four tortuous turns, and travelers had to make about six and one-half complete circles in less than four miles. The new roadway reduced the number of curves to eleven. The cost of about $425,000 was also financed and regulated by the National Industrial Recovery Act. In 1938, reconstruction of the remaining section of road to Buellton took out nineteen curves, and four reinforced concrete bridges (two of which were replacements) were part of the agreement. This work was done by the C.O. Sparks & Mundo Engineering Company. The cost for this federal aid project was approximately $307,000.

The road through Gaviota was to undergo major "face-lifting and concrete surgery" in the 1950s, when it was converted into four lanes of limited-access freeway. Completion dates for the different sections were: Las Cruces to the Gaviota (Nojoqui) Summit, November 1951; Gaviota Pass to Las Cruces, August 1952; Gaviota Pass Tunnel and approaches,

A modern, two-lane highway approaches Gaviota Pass, circa 1950.

May 1953; Gaviota Summit to the Santa Ynez River, February 1956; and Gaviota to Arroyo Hondo, July 1956. At a cost of $3 million, this replaced what was considered to be one of the most "tortuous" stretches of U.S. Highway 101. Of special interest was the section through Gaviota Pass, which was said to be one of the few locations, if not the only location in the United States, where a historical plaque commemorated an event that did *not* take place—the Frémont ambush.

Gaviota Pass Tunnel and Rest Areas
There were two ways to provide for the freeway through the narrow section of the gorge in the Gaviota Land. The first was to widen the fissure by removing thousands of tons of rock from the mountainside, but there was no nearby place to put the huge amount of material, and long hauls were not economical. The cost would have been more than twice that of the alternative, which was to drive a tunnel through, and of special importance was the fact that this choice would preserve the natural features of the area.

Bids were therefore opened in June 1951, and construction started in July on a 435-foot tunnel, which would be used by northbound traffic;

The north portal of the Gaviota tunnel nears completion.

southbound travelers would commute on the existing two-lane highway. Rhoades-Shofner Construction Company, of Los Angeles, was awarded the contract for $460,000, although actual costs were higher because of unanticipated requirements. The pass was the center of numerous faults; the largest was the Santa Ynez. The sandstone was not stable and required extensive supports; construction had to proceed with caution.

The first stage of tunnel construction required the establishment of a "working face," and the removal of rock had to be done from the south end only, as eliminated material from the north portal would have had to go across the creek and onto the existing highway at a point that was dangerous to traffic because of restricted view. The curved tunnel was to be thirty-five feet wide, twenty-two feet high, and lined with eighteen inches of cement. Power poles had not been in the Gaviota Pass until they were required for the tunnel (J.J. Hollister had sought to restrict them). Fluorescent lamps were used as they were considered to have low-power consumption, long life, and high illumination. One row was used at night, and two additional ones were required during daylight hours. They were installed by the Edward H. Anderson Electric Company.

The tunnel was "holed through" in February 1952. When drilling was

The south portal of the Gaviota tunnel today.

done from both ends, two men customarily shook hands through the opening; but as this underpass had to be drilled from one side only, there was debate over whether the "holing through" was achieved when the first ray of light was visible or when the opening was wide enough to crawl through. Rains and high velocity winds of up to seventy miles per hour delayed the construction, but it was completed in May 1953.

In March 1978, a rock slide of about two tons imperiled the highway, and although traffic was not actually fully halted, the threat of more slides prompted a closer investigation of the steep rock walls. The tunnel lighting was replaced in April 1985 at a cost of $230,000, and a bypass was required while the work was in progress.

Rock scaling was done north of the tunnel in November 1987 to remove loose boulders which could tumble down during heavy storms. Some "suspect" stones were pried loose, and traffic had to be stopped at intervals to allow for their removal. Two teams of men worked in different areas but at the same elevation to prevent rocks from being pushed down on others. Each worker was held by ropes tied at the top of the slope. A large crew was required to handle the slope work, removal, and traffic control. The endeavor started on October 26 and was completed on November 4, 1987, at a cost of about $13,000.

In August 1990, it was proposed to cover the area north of the tunnel with steel-cable fencing and netting as a preventative measure, which would help prevent boulders from plunging down the hillside and onto the road. Sometimes a driver coming around the tunnel curve had to swerve suddenly in order to avoid obstructions. The 1,700-foot fence would be able to stop a five-ton rock, and steel netting would be draped along the mountainside where fences could not be installed. A sixty-foot fence was erected north of the tunnel to gather opinion before a required county hearing, and Caltrans began installation of the $1.6 million rock-fall protection project in October 1992. It was one of the first and largest such projects in the nation.

Fallen rocks obstruct the road in front of the Gaviota tunnel.

Two rest areas were built at Gaviota Pass in January 1968. These were the first in Santa Barbara County, constructed by Harms Brothers at a cost of $209,222 in federal funds. The gorge was considered a majestic location, where thousands of motorists stopping daily would have a picturesque view of the historic pass as they traveled on El Camino Real. Separate facilities were constructed for both the northbound and southbound

Northbound rest area at Gaviota Pass.

lanes, designed to blend with the existing land formations. Buildings were faced with stone in order to harmonize with the natural rock, and each rest area provided water, restrooms, and picnic tables. The bronze Frémont plaque in the northbound rest area has been viewed daily by hundreds of travelers.

Other Changes

The retaining wall at Gaviota Creek was severely undercut by storm waters and was rebuilt in 1979 for $15,000. A new bridge and approaches were constructed in 1986 to improve the horizontal alignment; the cost was around $1,500,000.

The new intersection at U.S. 101 on the Chevron-Texaco project, Mariposa Reina (Butterfly Queen), was also under construction in the late 1980s. The design allowed for future highway expansion to six lanes, and the project was financed by Chevron and their partners at an estimated cost of $3 million, with right of way to be given to the state. Relentless rains on March 18, 1991, caused mudslides on the interchange, and the very heavily traveled Highway 101 had to be closed in both directions.

Replacing railings under the Indian's chin.

Another major project in the Gaviota Land came in April 1990, when Granite Construction Company won a large contract for $3.1 million to resurface both the northbound and southbound lanes of Highway 101 from Gaviota to the top of the grade. The project also included the re-paving of the rest areas and other work, including the installation of new bridge railings in the southbound lanes directly under the "Indian's chin" in the narrowest part of the pass. Concrete barriers were temporarily used for highway safety.

State Highway 1 between Las Cruces and Rancho San Julian was re-aligned in 1967-8 to eliminate forty-six curves, and this project included four bridges and a major intersection at Las Cruces. It was this construc-tion that was responsible for the elimination of the remaining business life in this small community. It was completed in May at a cost of $5.5 million, and federal funds provided approximately 60 percent of the finances.

Approximately eighteen miles of State Highway 1 between Las Cruces and Lompoc were officially designed a scenic corridor in 1972. The road went from the old adobe stage station and steel bridge at Las Cruces, crossed a picturesque canyon and two creeks, and continued over other

117

streams, rolling grass-covered hills, and open farm land without signs or billboards. Lompoc was considered to be the "Flower Seed Capital of the World," and a sign at the junction directed travelers a short distance to La Purísima Mission, regarded the most extensively restored of the twenty-one Spanish missions.

Despite these numerous road changes and alignments, the high speed of the myriad travelers winding through the Gaviota Pass has resulted in many collisions. Speed is now restricted to forty-five miles per hour in the southbound lanes approaching the pass, and extra-large warning signs with flashing lights have been placed on both sides of the road to alert drivers to the caution still needed in the pass.

Thousands of cars race daily through the Gaviota Land on U.S. Highway 101, one of the busiest freeways in the state. The highway has become one of the two most heavily traveled routes between Los Angeles and San Francisco, and when the southern section of Interstate 5 is closed, Highway 101 is the only other viable transportation avenue north from the enormous Los Angeles area.

Speeding traffic still has difficulty negotiating a bend of El Camino Real.

CHAPTER 9
Las Cruces

Roads greatly affected Las Cruces. They were responsible for its establishment, and they also quietly removed it, but this small community in the Gaviota Land was very much a part of its history. The name Las Cruces (the crosses) was thought to have been given by Franciscan friars when they found unmarked grave mounds and placed wooden crucifixes over them. The designation is also considered to indicate "crossroads," as two major routes intersected at Las Cruces. The creeks in that location also converge in a cross configuration. The west fork of Gaviota Creek, Las Cruces Creek, Las Canovas Creek, and hot springs drainages flow into Gaviota Creek to go through the Gaviota Pass to the ocean.

The Adobe
The 8,152-acre Las Cruces Rancho was granted to Miguel Cordero in 1836 by Governor Chico, then in 1837 by Governor Alvarado. The land had formerly been under the jurisdiction of the Santa Inés Mission. Cordero, born May 7, 1795, was a soldier from the Santa Barbara Presidio, and his father had been in Portolá's expedition. His adobe was thought to have been built around 1833, and he planted a garden, vineyard, and orchard along with developing fields of wheat and barley. Herds of cattle and sheep grazed on his rancho. But there were impediments to retaining the grant. Cordero died in March 1851 without a will. His widow, Maria Antonia, did not understand English and did not file with the Board of Land Commissioners for protection of her claim. She died in 1858, also intestate, and title went to the children in undivided interests. When Congress passed the Homestead Act in 1862, the Las Cruces area was

again available, since no claim had been filed.

The Corderos' children submitted petitions to Congress in 1876 requesting patents, and other citizens wrote letters in their support. The case came before a district court, and their grant was confirmed on August 31, 1880. The land was surveyed and a patent was finally approved on July 7, 1883. Large portions of the land had already been sold, however. Financial debts had necessitated the sales, and Hollister and the Dibblees were the principal buyers. They owned the majority of the Las Cruces land by 1876. Vicente Cordero, the oldest son, sold another interest to them for $2,218 on June 28, 1880, and Stanley and Juan Cordero sold Hollister additional acreage in 1927.

Cordero's adobe is extant, but as his nine children grew up, other adobe homes were also erected in the area. Between 1857 and 1876, probably six others were added, although the history and sites of these are not definite. The land on which the Las Cruces adobe stands went to Cordero's son, Juan, and then was sold to A.B. Williams. It is not certain who built the adobe that became the combination stage station, hotel, saloon, cafe, stable, and blacksmith shop. It was even hinted that at one time it was also a "house of ill repute" or a "hook shop." It has been said that Las Cruces was once considered a colorful "naughty town," full of women, gambling, and whiskey.

The adobe at Las Cruces was similar to others of the time, and there was another identical building at Gaviota (Miguel Burke's). Two or three rows of field stone with mortar formed the foundation, and walls were bricks bound with straw and mortar. Four parts lime to one part sand and water was the whitewash. Doors and window frames were set in place before the walls were built so that they adhered to the framing as they dried. The exterior walls were two feet thick, interior dividing walls were less, and ceilings varied.

Various people were in the adobe area. Frank L. Birabent leased the surrounding land for cattle in 1860. Pedro Baron also grazed stock. The Williams brothers were also there in the 1860s.

In anticipation of getting the stage franchise, the Las Cruces adobe was modified. A second partition, a fireplace, and a bar were built inside, and wallpaper was added. Wooden exterior rooms were constructed for ad-

The Las Cruces adobe, one-time stage stop, hotel, and saloon.

ditional bedrooms, and a barn and corrals were erected outside. These changes are believed to have been made by the Williams brothers. (In subsequent years, several roofs were laid over each other.)

The fourth brother, Alfred Bascom Williams, resided in the adobe in 1866, managing stages. He was also the deputy sheriff, constable, justice of the peace, and postmaster. Postal pay was $1 a month, payable in stamps. Williams didn't actually hold court trials, but he listened to both sides of a dispute and tried to make a just decision. The adobe was also a polling place; the first precinct of the third township was relocated from the Santa Inés Mission to Las Cruces in 1869. Williams moved to Santa Barbara to become county clerk, an ex-officio recorder and auditor; he sold his interest in Las Cruces to Thomas Dibblee for $3 an acre.

Robert J. Broughton was appointed postmaster in Las Cruces in 1869 and again in 1876. He managed the adobe inn and later also became the sheriff of Santa Barbara. His postmark read:

R. J. BROUGHTON
Dealer in
GROCERIES, BOOTS, SHOES, ETC.
Las Cruces
Santa Barbara Co. Cal.

Loustalot's stable. Fernando Librado is believed to be in the foreground.

There were not many postal duties from 1870 to 1872, as the stage company had breached its contract, and no mail was delivered or picked up; nevertheless, Las Cruces was still considered the only post office in the third township of Santa Barbara County. The stage route and mail again went through Gaviota and Las Cruces when a new postal contract was negotiated around 1873. Some other postmasters were Henry Dibblee, 1876; Miguel Burke, 1878; and Henry McNealy, 1882. The post office was discontinued on August 5, 1887, and opened again on October 18, 1889, and there is thought to have been a Los Cruces post office from September 1889 to February 1890 under postmaster James Donahue. This was described as being thirty-four miles west of Santa Barbara, while the Las Cruces post office was thirty-two miles away.

Jacob Loustalot, a Basque sheepherder, and his wife, Rose (née La Boucherie), rented the adobe from the Hollisters in 1894, and additional corrals were built to contain the many sheep and cattle that were driven through Las Cruces, some of which were headed to the slaughterhouse in Ellwood. The building was still a stage stop, cafe, and bar. Eight men could sleep inside, and others could stay in the barn. Such items as overalls were

The barn by the Las Cruces adobe, built with timbers from the Gaviota wharf.

available, the food was good, and numerous ranch hands stopped for meals. Rose's chicken dumplings were considered excellent cuisine.

The Loustalot family tells of the time Jacob was driving his sheep through the Gaviota Pass at the turn of the century. The driver of an approaching automobile didn't wish to stop and wait for the slow animals to mosey by. This must have frustrated Jacob, who took things into his own hands. He roped the man to the steering wheel until his herd had sauntered past, and the driver had to linger whether he wanted to or not.

Fernando Librado, a Santa Inés Mission Chumash, was the Loustalots' sheepherder and handyman for over twenty years. He lived to be well over one hundred years old, and ethnologist John P. Harrington interviewed him extensively on Chumash culture for the Smithsonian Institution. Fernando often spent time in the nearby caves, where signs of fire still remain. One was called his "sitting cave," and Las Cruces School children later ate lunch in these caverns.

Jacob Loustalot died about 1916, and his wife moved away several years later. Other adobe occupants for short periods were Oliver Johnson, Vicente Ortega, and Frank Lugo. The structure was then used as a supply

The Hollister barn was destroyed by winds, January 1993.

area for the Hollister Ranch. A tack room was added for the storage of such items as branding irons, harnesses, and blacksmith tools. The large barn is thought to have been built with some of the lumber came from the old Gaviota wharf. The barn had two planks which were considered to be some of the largest ever segments of milled fir lumber (about thirty-six feet long, eighteen inches wide, and four inches thick). An enormous cluster of prickly pear cactus snuggled nearby still remains, but powerful storms and gusty winds blew down the historic old barn in January 1993.

The Developing Community

A miniature community emerged at Las Cruces, and at one time it was even considered to be a "principal town." Traffic to the Gaviota wharf contributed to its growth, as an overnight stopover was necessary to make the two-day trip from the Santa Ynez Valley. Farmers also came to the area and planted crops such as beans, hay, and corn. There was often another family living nearby to assist with the labor, and as many as twenty additional men could be needed for seasonal work. Other residents were cowboys, and most worked for Hollister. Families had gardens, orchards, and numerous farm animals. At least one dog was necessary, as wild animals often came around. There were also multitudinous rattlesnakes, and everyone was aware of the danger. A bedtime ritual was to wave a stick around under the bed to check for a coiled reptile.

Everyone knew everyone else, and old-timers remembered people as

124

"caring." When animals were butchered or crops harvested, the surplus was shared with others. Families went to church in a buggy or wagon, and outhouses, wood stoves, and kerosene lamps were part of life. All hot water had to be heated on the stove. Clothes were often washed in a tub which was rocked by hand, and scrubbing was done on a washboard. A bath was a soak in a galvanized tub, and a kitchen or other area had to be closed off for this purpose, since there were no bathrooms. Residents in this small, remote area purchased flour in hundred-pound sacks, baked their own bread, and churned their own butter. Food was kept cool in a wire-frame box covered with wet sacks. Meat was salted down or made into jerky.

One interesting inhabitant of Las Cruces was a famous mountain-lion hunter, Charlie Tant. Tant was tall and lean, a real mountain man. It was said that he could tell the difference between male and female lion tracks. He traveled with five or six well-trained dogs in a Dodge truck. He took the animals and a single-shot .22 into the mountains and came out days or weeks later with several lion pelts, then worth about $50 each in bounty. A bag of cornmeal was said to be food for both him and his dogs. The animals curled up with him at night to sleep. Tant shot the big cats after his dogs tracked and treed them, but first he tied up his dogs to prevent injury—they could be killed by a swipe from the paw of a wounded and raging lion. Tant was also hired to kill hundreds of coyotes that were rapidly multiplying in the area. In later years, Tant broke his leg near Sisquoc and had to crawl an interminable fifteen miles along the river to reach help. This man of the mountains went to Oregon one winter and was caught in a big snow storm. He was given up for dead—but in spring, out he came!

The story is often repeated in Las Cruces of the time that Tant and Francis Matz caught a bobcat, crammed it into a suitcase, and placed it by the roadside. The brakes of an oncoming car screeched to bring it to an abrupt halt, the bag was snatched, and the vehicle proceeded down the road. A short distance away, however, brakes again shrieked, and bodies exploded out in all directions—the suitcase had been opened!

Gypsies came to Las Cruces and camped, but they were not considered welcome as they often stole chickens and picked fruit and berries. This was thought to be a time for residents to be "careful of possessions," and people were afraid young children might be kidnapped. Many of the wanderers, however, were said to be beautiful women and handsome men. They wanted to tell fortunes and would do so for ten cents. Hobos, the "knights of the road" with rolled packs on their backs, also traveled through, seeking food. It was reported that a circus even passed through the area at one time, putting on a show for the small community while en route to another location.

A massive woodcutting operation by the Union Commission Company of Santa Barbara took place at Las Cruces in 1910-20, when a great many of the old oak trees were taken off the land. There were immense demands for wood, both for cooking and for heating, and the railroad also used massive quantities.

Gas and electricity were not available until the late 1920s. When Johns Manville (later Manville Corporation and Celite Corporation) required additional gas in about 1926, a line from the Ellwood field was built through Las Cruces and Rancho San Julian to their plant near Lompoc. Gas was also piped to some ranch houses that were within a mile of the line, and the residents were given free gas refrigerators, stoves, and lights—major improvements.

Water. The hot springs in Las Cruces (often called the Gaviota Hot Springs) are located up the hill in a ravine of oaks and sycamores. The water flows through the earth's heated interior and bubbles into a natural rock-lined pool about ten feet across and three feet deep, which was dug during the Depression by the Works Progress Administration (W.P.A.). The sulfur plunge became a bathtub for early residents, and Saturday nights were special. The main spring gushes about five hundred gallons an hour, with a temperature around ninety degrees.

Many residents of Las Cruces in the early years used sulfur water for drinking as well as for other uses. In early times, it was hauled in wagons by horses and had to settle at least overnight. It was later piped down Las Canovas Creek in a wooden trough to residents, and pipelines subsequently replaced the trough. This water was also pumped to Las Cruces Canyon for irrigation. (There were additional sulfur springs years ago at Refugio, which bubbled up a few feet from the beach. This was discovered

126

Las Cruces Hot Springs, circa 1945.

when the Shell Oil Company drilled for oil with a shaft of more than 1,700 feet. Sulfur springs were found instead, and a pool was made for individual use. The springs were later closed off.)

A massive amount of water arrived from a "higher source" one year. A cloudburst cut down through the canyon by the hot springs, and although it didn't last long, it left a visible scar on the hill where it struck. Caroline Henning saw this large gush of water cut a gully down the mountain where there hadn't been one before, flooding its way to Gaviota Creek and the ocean.

Las Cruces School. The Las Cruces School was a one-room structure built in 1880-81. It was also sometimes used as a church for Mass, and occasionally for dances. It stood near a large oak tree across the road from the adobe. The building was destroyed by fire in 1907, and a second structure, then considered one of the largest one-room educational facilities in the county, was constructed west of the original location. The yard was fenced, and there was an outhouse in each back corner. From twelve to fifteen children were there in 1920, and an average daily attendance of at least six had to be maintained to keep it open. The teacher lived in a

127

Teachers and students of the original Las Cruces School.

Las Cruces School as rebuilt in 1907.

small, wooden building not far from the adobe.

Children walked to school if possible, but many rode horses or ponies, and the animals required food, water, and containment until the return trip home. Sometimes a cart pulled by two horses was transportation. More than an hour was required for some students to reach school (especially before the San Julian School came into existence around 1910). After the Vista Del Mar Union School District was established, the school was torn down in the late 1930s, and it is said that some of the lumber was used for the dairy on the Rancho San Julian.

The Las Cruces Inn and Other Businesses

In 1910, Charlie Nichols and his wife, Frances (née Vascuez), owned the Las Cruces Inn, which had been built by Las Cruces carpenter, John Henning. The structure was located right next to the road, and a sign nearby announced "Rancho Foods." A wooden bridge was first built across the creek for access, but when the road changed, a steel bridge in another location replaced it. The inn had a large kitchen, a combination dining and living room, and three bedrooms plus four more in another building across the road. There were also several storerooms in the rear and a dance hall with a stage. Next to the inn was a large fig tree and a massive cluster of blackberries. There was a garden for vegetables, but produce was also grown on Nichols's property up the road near his orchard (later removed for road changes). A large redwood tree stood in back of the inn and still remains, but it is broken off and struggling for existence (an antenna was even placed on top of it at one time).

A great deal of work was required to manage a hostelry, and extra help was needed. Washing sheets and laundry had to be done by hand. Ice was delivered for an ice box. Cows were milked daily, butter was churned, and fruit was canned. Turkeys, chickens, and pigs were raised, killed, and cooked. Pastries, cakes, bread, and pies were homemade, a dozen or more at one time. Nichols also had a little adobe house up the hill from the sulfur springs, on a place called "Charlie's Flat," or "Squat." (It was actually "squatted" by the Savage family which had lived and run cattle there, and Nichols acquired it from them.) Nichols had some beautiful white-haired goats and several donkeys. Hunters would some-

Two views of the Las Cruces Inn.

The Feliz family in front of the Las Cruces Inn: parents Joseph and Eliza; children Bee, Ida, Vernie, Jack, and Margie.

times stay overnight in his one-room structure, and the donkeys were referred to as "the squad" when they periodically rambled down the hill—sometimes, it was said, with jingling bells.

Nichols later leased the inn to others. Mr. and Mrs. Joseph Feliz were there from 1921 through 1922. Joseph was considered a professional cowboy; Eliza Feliz was the principal manager with the help of her daughters, but serving meals at all hours finally made it necessary to hire a daytime cook. A "stage" driver was given a shopping list for groceries at Newland's Gaviota Store or Nielson's in Solvang. The list was left at the establishments, and in a couple of days, the driver brought back both groceries and mail. This "stage" or speed wagon was a gasoline-powered vehicle with two passenger seats on each side and a closed compartment behind the driver for mail and cargo.

Andy Lynn and his wife ran the hotel for several years; Stan and Peggy Humphries took it over in 1936 and ran it through World War II, with the help of their two daughters, May and Grace, who helped serve customers by waiting on tables, plucking chickens, etc. The Humphries

131

Saddle bar stools at the Las Cruces Inn.

converted the master bedroom into a bar when Prohibition ended. The saloon was especially remembered for saddles on the stools. Good meals were served. The inn itself had five tables, and a den seated another six customers. The banquet room had a forty-person capacity, and the dance hall could accommodate almost one hundred people. The Highway Patrol held monthly tri-county meetings there, with from sixty to ninety people in attendance. World War II soldiers were also served Christmas dinner in the dance hall.

The inn was later sold to Andrew Cipollo, and in the 1950s it was purchased for around $10,000 by Dr. A. E. Serns and his wife, Millie. They received clear title and later sold to the state, but a Santa Barbara lawyer who handled the sale was involved in a swindle of monies in the transaction. Road changes erased the inn in 1967. When the state took over the land for construction of the wide interchange between Highway 101 and Highway 1, the intention was to leave the inn as a memory of the past, but it was destroyed when the man who bulldozed the area made a mistake and demolished it.

Juan Flores operated the dirt-floor blacksmith shop where horses were shoed and machinery was sharpened. Spurs and bits for horses were made, sometimes with gold and silver inlays. Flores used the hard steel from old horseshoes, and his bits were known all around as the "Las Cruces bit."

He also did "tiring." Wagon wheels were too big to fit into a forge for re-pairs. They had a wooden "tire" around a steel rim, and when vibrations loosened it, re-fitting was necessary. Corn cobs were placed around the rim and ignited with a flammable fuel. After the metal expanded, the cobs were removed, and the alloy shrank to fit the wood as it cooled. Flores's wife, Christina, rented rooms and was a well-known midwife. She was also famous for her tamales and enchiladas, which were purchased by those in the community as well as travelers.

Up the canyon, the ranch land to the left of Highway 1 was once owned by Joe Bartaloza. Tony Prevedello, a dairy owner in Santa Barbara, later acquired that section. The Dibblees sold some land in 1952 to Garth Flint, who built two houses on the hill in that area. Other owners were the Bazzi brothers, Dale Van Avery, and Adolph (Pete) and Helen Pedotti.

The roads through Las Cruces greatly controlled community life. As they changed, businesses and homes were also rearranged. When the highway from Lompoc was first shifted in Las Cruces, the Loustalots built a bar, restaurant, and barn near the new road. Although it was predomi-nantly a rooming house for working men, serving mostly railroad workers, travelers also stopped there and could get care for their animals. The busi-ness sign read: "Jacob Loustalot Hotel and Bar—Meals 25 cents." When the road changed, patronage dwindled, and the property was sold. The Loustalots also put in a small service station just beyond the inn, which was operated by Frank Town.

Road modifications required the relocation of the Nichols's dance hall, and he repositioned it further north, converting it into a home; the kitchen was on the stage area. Nichols also built a gas station in that vi-cinity, which Ed Erickson operated. Snacks and a few groceries were also sold. Walter (Valdemar) Nielsen first had a garage in the basement of the Nichols property and purchased acreage up the road to build a Richfield-Shell service station; a stucco home, which was later beautifully land-scaped, was constructed in 1928. Trucks coming fast down the Nojoqui grade, however, sometimes overturned in their yard, dumping lettuce or tomatoes everywhere. Weekly stops to their home were made by vendors: fresh fish, Helm's bakery goods, Chris Madsen's fresh vegetables, Frank Fitzgerald's milk delivery, and front door laundry and dry-cleaning service.

Jack Chester (left) and Walter Nielsen at Nielsen's Las Cruces garage.

One summer a terrible odor came across the road from their garage. Investigation revealed a decomposed body hanging from an oak tree.

Walter and Pauline Nielsen had three children—Beverly, Ronald, and Merlin. They left in 1946 to move to Tucson, and their business was leased to Jack Chester and later the Cerielli family from Santa Barbara. The state took over the land in the 1950s for road modifications, and the garage was demolished. The residence was sold to Abbie Donahue. It was then moved close to the intersection of Highway 1 and Highway 101 and restored by her sons, Thomas and William, but the state later condemned this property also and took it over in another road change.

Loustalots' Store

After Highway 101 was built, Rose Loustalot built another roadside business in 1917 to service the increasing automobile traffic. This was a store with attached cafe and service station, which became the famous general store on the highway. John Henning, carpenter for the inn, also built the store. (His death in later years was rather unusual: at the age of ninety-five, he just left his home in Las Cruces one afternoon and disappeared. He was never found, and no one knew what happened to him.)

The Loustalots' Las Cruces Store.

The Loustalot business was first operated by Rose's oldest son, Pierre (Pete), and then by the Barnses. Pete's sister, Justine Meloling and her husband, Albert, took it over for a while, and it was then leased to William H. (Hubbard) Moffett in the 1920s. (He and a partner had previously operated a store at Tajiguas, and he had also been a station agent there and at Gaviota.) Eugene Hess managed an auto repair business in back of the store in 1927, and his wife, Marguerita (née Tico) was Moffett's clerk and bookkeeper. They lived in the one-bedroom house in back.

Moffett left Las Cruces around 1931 to open an enterprise at Orella, and the Hesses leased the store until 1938. Eugene also purchased property from the Dibblees and built a garage nearby. Part of it was converted into a gunsmith shop. A wooden platform was constructed and rented to the county as a produce-inspection station, and large trucks were required to stop for checks. Wilburn Sherrill, one of the inspectors, lived in the house in back of the store.

When the Hesses left in 1938, John and Cesarina Loustalot came to Las Cruces to take over their business. John had been a partner in the Johnson Garage in Santa Barbara, but he had been born in the Las Cruces adobe (1899) and had gone to school there. He and his wife purchased

The Las Cruces garage.

the garage from Hess. John also had an orchard across the road, almost adjacent to that of Nichols, given to him by his mother around 1910. It contained some of the large, old fruit trees planted years ago by Spanish families and a nearby cabin.

In earlier days, clothing such as overalls, jeans, shirts, and socks had been sold at the store, but food, drinks, and gas became commodities required by automobile travelers. The store had a country atmosphere inside. Deer antlers on the wall looked down at a display of antiques. Several stools edged a counter, and there were accommodations in a side room. Front porch benches provided additional seating, and there was a picnic area behind the garage. Regular food deliveries were made, and Weber's Bakery delivered almost daily. Beer was available too, and a small room previously used for garage supplies was converted into a liquor store.

Mail arrived at Las Cruces addressed: "Las Cruces via Gaviota" or "Las Cruces/Gaviota." It was delivered for pick-up by local residents and placed on a shelf or in slots, where it remained until claimed; thus it was possible for some people to "notice" the mail of others. The store had a telephone exchange, and fifty cents a day was paid for its operation. Even when the store was closed, travelers stopped and communicated through an intercom. There were also many accidents, and the Highway Patrol was often in contact. Frequent calls on the party line (one long and two short rings) were forewarnings of wrecks.

The Loustalots had two children, Jeannette and Jean, and lived in the residence in back of the store, which had a kitchen, two bedrooms, and a large dining/living room combination; another bedroom and an enclosed lattice patio were added later. Managing the business, however, required additional assistance, and Harvey McGuire was one of the Loustalots' helpers. McGuire lived just up the canyon and was said to have a special relationship with wild animals. Tex was another employee. One time, during gas rationing days, a driver requested a large quantity of fuel and refused to pay, saying he had only asked for a dollar's worth. When he drove off, John and Tex chased after him and a fight ensued, but the money was obtained, although John had a chipped tooth as a reminder of the episode.

The store became the local recreation area for the military men camped near the beaches during World War II. It had a pinball machine and jukebox for musical entertainment, and permission was obtained from the sheriff for two slot machines. The Army Signal Corps was at Gaviota, bivouacked in the Associated Oil Company buildings, and other military were at Refugio. There was also a station near Cojo and a prison camp not far from El Capitan. Big guns were all along the coast to defend the important railroad and the trestles, and to monitor offshore activity. The military police also stopped by the store in order to try to trace Army escapees from Camp Cooke (now Vandenberg Air Force Base).

One interesting incident occured when a trestle guard captured on a movie camera a gopher being swallowed by a gopher snake, which, in turn, was being attacked by a king snake. The whirring of the camera made the king snake think a rattle snake was after him, and so he disgorged the gopher snake, who released the gopher. This incident in the Gaviota Land became part of Ripley's *Believe It or Not!*

Numerous travelers and many buses stopped at the little store, both coming and going. There were ten to twelve there at one time. Large buses with soldiers from Camp Cooke stopped by each Saturday morning on the way out and Sunday night on the way back; others from Camp Roberts were also there. A "sea" of soldiers was sometimes eating outside the establishment, and it could require as many as ninety loaves of bread to make hundreds of sandwiches. These were either made the night before or early in the morning, and the buses sometimes called in orders ahead of time. The building was also a flag stop for the Greyhound Bus, although tickets were not sold there, and people going to Alisal Ranch were also met at the Loustalots' store.

The Loustalots were also wardens for blackouts during World War II. Residents were required to turn off lights and pull down shades when enemy attacks were expected, and this occurred many times in Gaviota, as there was frequent concern about movements in the ocean nearby. Blackout lights were required for any night driving that could not be avoided. People were especially frightened when a submarine of the Japanese Imperial Navy's Sixth Fleet emerged down the coast east of the Gaviota Land and fired on the Ellwood oil fields. It was the first attack of the war on the continental United States. The shots were fired at about 7 P.M. on February 23, 1942, just as President Franklin Roosevelt was speaking to the nation in a fireside chat, and they continued for more than thirty minutes.

Although not a great deal of serious damage was done, people were petrified of another attack. A blackout was ordered for almost 100 miles, and the Army shut off radio stations so that enemy forces could not gain locational directions. After the shelling, the submarine headed west toward Gaviota and disappeared. Some of the shells that landed in the foothills were duds, and a few of them still in the chaparral exploded during the big fire in 1955.

During this scare, two large military buses pulled up to the Las Cruces store one day and literally took over everything, including the telephone. They set up camp for about 100 men and stayed for several weeks, providing their own facilities for eating and sleeping. There was concern because several vehicles had recently been stopped for inspection and Japanese had been found hiding under tarps. The sheriff had also discovered special radio equipment in the residence of at least one Japanese.

During the war, entertainers and movie stars traveling to Camp Cooke and other bases also stopped along this lonely stretch of road in the Gaviota Land. Cesarina Loustalot told about the day a gentleman came

Autographs from Cesarina Loustalot's scrapbook.

into the store asking about repairs for his car, and a lovely lady came in behind him. It was Lucille Ball! Other famous visitors were Clark Gable, Red Skelton, Janet Gaynor, Bob Hope, Jimmy Durante, and Shirley Temple and her first husband, John Agar. Cesarina kept a scrapbook of their signatures. Other well-known people stopped at Nielsen's service station and garage, located further north on the opposite side of the road. Their movie camera captured Johnny Morris, the radio celebrity who "called for Philip Morris" cigarettes.

The store frequently served breakfast to many of the men working on the Gaviota tunnel, some of whom even camped in back of the store. A party was held at the completion of the tunnel, and the "guest of honor" was a barbecued wild pig. But a sad note was that the engineer in charge of the construction was killed in an auto accident a short time later.

John Loustalot had an accident in his orchard in 1949 while operating a tractor, and lost the use of one leg. He and his wife left the store in 1957 and moved to Santa Ynez. The business was leased to the Standard Oil Company for $900 a month, and they subleased it to Lee Wills. When the wide intersection was constructed at Las Cruces in 1967, the state

Construction of the new Vista de Las Cruces School.

condemned the property and appropriated it for $85,000. The business was then demolished under bulldozers, gone forever.

The state also purchased land from the Hollister Company and other land holders and became the new owners of the hot springs, remaining barn, adobe, and steel bridge at Las Cruces—the last remnants of the once-thriving community. The adobe is thought to be one of only three in California that are state-owned prototypes of early stage stations, and it has been deemed eligible for the National Register of Historic Places. The state has placed a metal roof over it, but no other improvements have been made, and the building has been extensively vandalized. Discussions have been held about its restoration, but what is left now of the crumbling structure does not reveal a ghost of the life that was once there.

Roads established the community of Las Cruces in the Gaviota Land; later they shoved it around, and finally they devoured it. The business and residential community of Las Cruces is now only a memory of the past, but a large new school with a new name, Vista de Las Cruces (formerly Vista Del Mar) sprawls over the heart of the land. There will now be a different life in a forgotten area.

CHAPTER 10
Hollister Ranch and Gaviota Store

After the Hollister-Dibblee partnership was dissolved, the coastal section of the Gaviota Land from Arroyo Hondo to Cojo belonged to the Hollisters, and hundreds of white-faced Hereford cattle with the adjoining "W" and "H" brand grazed on this extensive coastal strip. Ranch operations were similar to those on Rancho San Julian, but horses rode on the beach. The "bloody hide" method was employed for rounding up cattle: instead of herders working for weeks to locate animals in the hills, the hide of a freshly-slain bull was hung from a post, and other steers were immediately attracted to it. Large roundups were busy times when animals were separated for sale, branded, and vaccinated. Corrals were built in various areas of the vast ranch to handle the extensive herds. The Las Cruces corral in the flat land by the adobe has vanished with time, but segments of the Gaviota corral on the west side of the canyon still remain, a reminder of those former days.

Most of the ranch hands lived on the ranch with their families, and a school was established at Drake for the children. The cattle-dipping area for the ranch was in Las Cruces Canyon (the cement boiler pits were removed in later years), and an immense walnut orchard was also there.

When Hollister died in August 1886, the acreage was held by the Estate of W.W. Hollister. The ranch was idle or leased until 1910, when the Hollister Estate controlled the real estate, and Hollister's son, J.J. (Jim) Hollister, took over management of the large-scale cattle operations.

Gaviota Store
The old Gaviota Store on the coastal bluff to the east of the beach was

Cattle from Hollister Ranch on the beach near Gaviota.

Hollister Ranch at Gaviota.

part of the ranch and also important to others in the Gaviota Land. The Hollister family owned the land, built the store, and leased out the management. Frank Newland was the first proprietor in about 1916. (He later became a chiropractor in Santa Barbara.) The Buhn brothers, Otto and Walter, followed in the 1920s, remaining through most of World War II. Newton Moffitt leased the operation from 1944 to 1949; he had been a

Hollister Ranch buildings at Las Cruces.

former custodian of Vista Del Mar School, and his wife, Lucy, was the county librarian at Gaviota, operating a branch out of a room in the custodian's house. James Fitzgerald managed the store from 1949 to 1959, and Newton Foster succeeded him.

The store was an unofficial ranch headquarters and a mecca in the area. It was also a mini-emporium for the numerous railroad employees living nearby, providing food, clothing, and gas, along with other items, and special orders were also taken. Punch boards made popular games: holes in them were stuffed with pieces of paper which designated prizes, and for ten cents a chance, a box of candy, a watch, a rifle, or some other treasure might be won.

The first store building had been by the old road, close to the railroad tracks; but when the road moved, the store did too. The front entrance had to be changed to the side when the gas pumps were expanded. The large building could also serve as a dance hall. Records were generally played, but "live" entertainment was sometimes available. At one time, there was an old barber's chair, which had come around the Horn in Gold Rush days; it was transferred to the store from the depot barber shop.

The store manager lived in a three-bedroom home in back of the building. There was also a nearby cottage and about ten auto courts, overnight quarters for early travelers, with bathrooms and kitchenettes as well

The old Gaviota Store, unofficial headquarters of Hollister Ranch.

as sleeping accommodations. Their era passed when more modern facilities became available, and they were not remodeled. Another nearby residence belonged to Harold and Ruth (née Bethune) Hollister. Rattlesnakes, 'possums, raccoons, and bats were also part of the neighborhood.

The telephone exchange was located in the store and served a vital function for the entire area, providing Hollister and other locals with a link to the rest of the world twenty-four hours a day. Incoming calls were directed by a combination of long and short rings. The ranch was often in contact with the railroad when thousands of cattle were to be sold on the market. The post office was also an integral part of the store and had its own corner of the building. Although not spacious, it provided all the necessary services, and U. S. inspectors came regularly to make sure it did. There were some thirty post office boxes, "Wanted" posters adorned the walls, and the sheriff and Highway Patrol often checked for escaped prisoners from Camp Cooke, especially during the war years.

Mail, separated by bags for Gaviota, Buellton, Solvang, Santa Ynez, and other areas, arrived daily at the Gaviota depot, and Gaviota's mail came to the store to be sorted into pouches for delivery to all those on the Star Route. Cooper, Sorensen, and Benson were some of the carriers; King and Wilson were among the station agents and telegraphers. Some of the postmasters at Gaviota were Amy McNealy, April 1896; Robert Compton, September 1901; Henry Remington, April 1905; Frank Therman, December 1906; George Wilson, July 1907; Walter Buhn, August 1926; Newton Moffitt, December 1944; and James Fitzgerald, December 1949. The small postal headquarters at the store closed in June 1957, but it was reactivated on August 1, 1957, as a rural station under Goleta, and Newton Foster was placed in charge.

The store became a popular "restaurant" along a lonely stretch of road. A cash register clutched the money, and dishes were scoured in a galvanized tub. The restaurant was especially well-liked by truck drivers. The kitchen was small, but the hamburgers, stew, and chili were famous. There were school-type desks with arms, arranged to give visitors a panoramic ocean view, and an eating counter was also available. The establishment was also a good meeting place. Dutch Wilson from Cojo and another rancher from Long Beach convened at the old Gaviota Store to exchange hogs for the varying of blood lines. Hobos and gypsies also were visitors.

At one time, a Fitzgerald employee was literally set on fire at the store. After closing the gasoline pumps late in the evening, Harold Davis was warming himself by the old heater when his clothes suddenly exploded in flames. He got to the back doorway, where Mrs. Fitzgerald saw the blazing employee and immediately grabbed a pair of scissors to cut away burning clothing. Davis was badly burned and was quickly taken to the hospital.

The 1955 Fire

The Fitzgeralds were at the Gaviota Store during the big fire in September 1955. It was one of the largest fires in the county's history, and it raged out of control for days. The inferno jumped Highway 101 near the store. Cars were stopped for miles; railroad trains were halted, and the store itself had to be evacuated twice. Long lines of people waited to get telephone calls through. When the electricity went out, provisions from the store's freezer were cooked to feed the weary firefighters. The inferno was not easy to fight. The rugged, rocky hills made it difficult to maneuver equipment, dry dense brush exploded into flames, and winds fanned the flames higher. Telephone poles continued to burn long after the conflagration had

145

passed, and large oak trees were left big blackened stalks.

In addition to local firemen, firefighters came from as far as San Luis Obispo and Ventura. Some of the men had close calls. Several thousand wooden railroad ties caught fire, and emergency crews had to first fight the flames before repairs could be made. Two bulldozer operators, cut off by flames, drove their machines together so they could crawl in-between. Men driving a water-filled cement mixer jumped inside and closed the lid. An early report indicated that a plane had crash-landed on the beach near Gaviota; turbulent weather in the vicinity, probably caused from the fire, had caused it to go down. Fortunately, it was later learned, it had landed without damage.

As the inferno continued to rage, animals ran to escape, but asphyxiation killed many of the smaller ones. The sheriff ordered the evacuation of campers at Gaviota Beach, but John McDonell and Carmen Nelson, the concessionaire and caretaker, remained. Concern was great enough, however, for them to carry furniture down to the beach to try to save it if the fire persevered in its course toward them. When the flames got close to the Gaviota Store, however, the direction of the wind changed, and the beach was no longer threatened. Afterward, however, soot and ashes covered everything, a reminder of the danger narrowly escaped.

This large fire in the Gaviota Land was remembered as a devastating event. It could be seen in the night all the way to Santa Barbara and caused concern even in Lompoc. It burned close to 98,000 acres, including everything along Highway 101 from Ellwood to Gaviota. Over a dozen homes and numerous other buildings were destroyed, but the firefighters succeeded in halting the inferno at Gaviota Pass. Dozens of fire engines and men converged on the area to wage a last-ditch stand and prevent the immense flames from leaping across Highway 101. The pass provided the needed firebreak. It was estimated that it had cost $800,000 to fight the blaze, which caused $4 million in damage.

The Ranch Is Sold
After J.J. Hollister died in 1961 at ninety-one, many years of family ownership ended, and the Winchester Canyon (940 acres), Salsipuedes (6,700 acres), and the Santa Anita/Gaviota (26,580 acres) parcels were sold to a

Los Angeles syndicate in 1964. The price was said to be in excess of $12 million, and it was estimated that sixty-seven heirs had to be notified. It was a major real estate transaction and had a year-long escrow.

The state purchased a large portion of the Las Cruces area in 1967, and Macco Corporation, a large, recreational land development company (subsidiary of the Penn-Central Company), purchased notes in 1968 covering the sale of the ranch to the syndicate. They bought a coastal section of over 14,000 acres for a reported $7.5 million. This included approximately seventeen miles of ocean frontage and forty-four acres in the old Gaviota Store vicinity, where there was to be a modern Gaviota Village. This was to be a "fishing village" and a tourist center with a historic museum. A 100-foot lighthouse/observation tower was to provide a sweeping view of the ocean and hills. At one time, an authentic working lighthouse was even considered.

The "fishing village" was to be part of a massive recreational complex on Hollister Ranch itself. It was to become a leisure wonderland, a kind of private national park. Plans called for a vast commercial and recreational area that would take five years or longer to develop. It was to include around 1,500 campsites, 200 cabañas (prefabricated cabins), and various recreation trails. A pier, centers for goods and services, water reservoirs, firefighting equipment, internal security, and sewage, water, and filtration plants would also be part of the network. Extensive use of the land was predicted for both day use and camping.

The recreation complex did not come into existence, however, although the landmark old Gaviota Store was torn down and a new service station and a building containing a restaurant, coffee shop, general store, and bar took its place—a vast change from the old establishment and the memories of the past. The tall lighthouse, however, was seen only on paper. More recently, a motel, shops, and an R.V. park next to the Gaviota Village have also been proposed.

In 1970, Macco sold the land to the Mortgage Guarantee Investment Corporation of Milwaukee, which did not feel it was economically feasible to undertake the recreational project. In 1971, the property was divided into 136 parcels of at least 100 acres each, which were priced from $100,000 to $400,000 and sold to individual buyers. Management was un-

147

Gaviota Village.

der the Hollister Ranch Owners Association. The large old Hollister manor, built around 1911, now served as a meeting place for the association. Pages of deed restrictions applied to the new owners: there could be no sub-dividing of parcels, and existing "forests and other designated growth" could not be removed. Title was held in undivided interests, and as many as five homes could be built on a single parcel, but they could only be occupied by the owner, non-paying guests, or employees.

The land became a working cattle ranch with several thousand head of cattle and limited residences. Animal management was by a ranch co-op in which each landholder held stock. Owners were paid for grazing privileges, but they could fence their land if they did not wish to participate. Taxes were low, as the land had been zoned as an agricultural preserve, and it was also considered a wildlife and plant reserve. Game flourished, and wild animals such as pigs, deer, bobcats, mountain lions, bears, foxes, skunks, and others lived in the vicinity. There were six different creeks, ten miles of paved roads, and more than one hundred miles of unpaved ones. Common areas included over eight miles of beaches and several cabañas for social activities. Roads were guarded and patrolled. The coast was legally open to the public, but geography prevented access, and this section of the coast remained secluded and private for the use of the privileged people living there. This land of sequestered individual parcels adjacent to Gaviota on the west is still known as the Hollister Ranch, or sometimes just "the ranch."

CHAPTER 11
Cojo and Channel Island Neighbors

Cojo

To the far west of the Gaviota Land, on the other side of Hollister Ranch, lies Cojo. Cojo is a large, relatively unoccupied, primitive ranching region of about 25,000 acres owned by the Bixby Ranch Company. Fred Bixby purchased 10,000 acres around 1911 and later acquired 15,000 adjoining acres of Jalama. He also had properties in other states, and his operations were managed centrally from Long Beach. Some of his Cojo supervisors were Steve Wilson and his son, Link (Lawrence); Ed Janeway, Bixby's son-in-law; and Brad Lundberg. Cojo has also had some well-known vaqueros. Link's brother, Dutch (Ray), came to Cojo in 1923 and was there for many years. Both Link and Dutch were said to be able to cut a single cow out of a crowded herd.

There were not many buildings on the Bixby Ranch—only a large barn, corrals, chutes, and homes for the men. Many supplies arrived by rail, and groceries and meat came daily at one time. Some of the cowboys were married and had families, but most were single and lived in the bunkhouse. Abundant and excellent meals came from the cook house, where cooking and baking were done on a wood stove. Sometimes even abalone or rabbit was available as an addition to the traditional breakfast.

Thousands of cattle often grazed on the hills, and trained horses were vital for ranch operations. They had to be able to respond immediately to commands, and they had to be surefooted in those hills dotted with holes from gophers and squirrels. Brahma bulls were bred, and spotted pinto horses were once promoted; but draft horses such as Shires, Belgians, and

149

Ranching at Cojo.

Cojo roundup: Dutch Wilson, far left; Link Wilson, foreground.

Dutch and Link Wilson.

Draft horses, a Cojo specialty.

151

Clydesdales were a specialty. There were about 350 of these animals at one time, and Bixby was one of the largest ranches in the United States breeding and raising these beautiful, powerful animals with deep bodies and heavy bones, considered the tallest of horses. The ranch had about six matched eight-horse teams of Shires, which were often taken to fairs (including the World's Fair at San Francisco) where they almost always took first prize.

Animal diseases were a special challenge in the early days. One year the ranch had a lot of wood ticks, and screw worms could always get into the skins of the animals. Chloroform had to be used to eradicate maggots. A terrible disease, "the strangles," killed many horses; it caused sores to form on their bodies and pus pockets on their wind pipes, slowly choking the animals to death.

Cattle and horses from the Bixby Ranch were shipped out by rail from the corrals at the Concepcion depot; mail also arrived there to be picked up for delivery. The blacksmith and his family lived in a house across from the depot, and some of the section crew stayed in railroad cars. A commissary and kitchen car provided supplies and food from rail deliveries. The depot was also a voting place for those on the Hollister and Bixby ranches. It was a time when people dressed up and were said to "whisper in small groups." There were both strong Democrats and Republicans in the precinct.

The wind and fog were often severe in Cojo, and sometimes horses refused "to go into it." Gales have been known to blow for weeks at a time, and some claimed it blew 360 days out of a year. Many times the wooden gate at the top of the ridge between Cojo and Jalama had to be opened and closed by a car, as a man was not strong enough to push it against the gales. Raising crops could also be difficult. A Chinese man planted a potato crop one year, and the wind blew most of the soil away, revealing all the spuds.

In the past, extensive whaling took place off the Cojo and Gaviota areas, and many petrified vertebrae have been found along this section of coast. Almost an entire whale was said to be located in the bank above the old whaling station at Cojo, and it was taken apart, bone by bone, for preservation in Berkeley.

Concepcion depot.

Some plans for the Cojo area never materialized. A large industrial city called Seabrook near Cojo and Point Conception was laid out and planned on paper in 1908. The North American Steel Mills were to be located there, as were other factories and foundries. This industrial city was only ever seen on a map, however. P.W. Murphy, the owner of Cojo Ranch in 1887, was going to plan a town and put a wharf at Cojo Bay if the railroad came up the coast. Although that was the chosen route for the rails, the town was not built; a couple of years later, Murphy lost the land through a foreclosure sale.

Pea Pickers. Hay was an early major crop on the Cojo Ranch; mustard produced a good yield during World War II and was sold to the military for gas. Beans were also planted, and peas yielded an abundant harvest in 1938-39. The first large pea-pickers' camp in northern Santa Barbara County was established at Cojo, where peas were to be picked and packed in the warehouse by the depot. Advertisements were placed all over the state for workers, and accommodations were made for about 1,200 laborers. Most of them were to reside in tents. Massive numbers arrived, but

153

they came in a year of heavy rains, and it was impossible to travel over the muddy roads to get into the area. Tractors dragged in many of them. Some camped at the Jalama turnoff while waiting to reach the peas, hanging out blankets and clothing on the fence to dry.

After they did get in, other downpours followed, and the workers were unable to leave. They were chilled, wet, miserable, and sick. Pneumonia and other diseases became prevalent. Food and medication had to be brought in, much of it by horseback. Dr. Larry Heiges, a Lompoc physician, came to care for the sick. It was a time of great hardship for those who had come miles for work. Eventually the peas did get harvested, but it took a long time and was a disaster which would not be forgotten.

The Lighthouse. Off the western corner of Cojo lies Point Conception, which is sometimes considered to be a division between northern and southern California. The lighthouse there with its "winking eye" has for years guided ships in navigating the sharp turn. The original brick tower was built atop the bluff in the 1850s, when materials were landed in the surf at Cojo Bay. The polished-crystal lens came from Paris, and it took several months to put it together after some of its parts were lost and others damaged in the landing. The lighthouse was rebuilt midway down the steep bluff in 1881 after an earthquake caused severe damage to the original structure. It was thought that the first tower had been up too high, causing the light to shine out upon layers of clouds.

The lighthouse complex consisted of the light tower, a foghorn, warehouse buildings, a double apartment house, two smaller dwellings, a barn, a tool shed, a carpenter shop, and a laundry. For many years, four families (superintendent and three assistants) lived on this lonely section of the coast, isolated from the rest of the world. Before the railroad arrived, supplies were brought in only about twice a year. Ships often had to anchor for several days until the sea was calm enough to send in tenders. A trip to Lompoc required two days and an overnight stay.

The lighthouse was at first lit by sperm whale oil, then by five-wick kerosene lanterns. Incandescent oil-vapor lamps were next, and a 1,000-watt incandescent lamp was installed in 1948. Rotation by pendulum weight changed to electricity-generated gears. The steam-operated dia-

The Point Conception lighthouse as rebuilt in 1881.

The Iowan, *beached off Government Point in 1941.*

phone of the fog bell was replaced with an electric foghorn, which sounded a two-second blast every thirty seconds. The Coast Guard took over the lighthouse in 1938, and it was automated in 1973, controlled from Point Arguello.

There have been numerous ships that have not perceived the warnings of the lighthouse's beacon shining over thrashing waters or the foghorn's warning cry echoing off the rocks. The *Iowan* was one vessel that came ashore next to Government Point in the fall of 1941. It was towed back out but first had to be lightened, and items flung overboard were found all over the shore.

The Bixby Ranch Company made plans to build 490 custom homes ranging in price from $500,000 to $1.5 million, a resort lodge, an equestrian center, and two golf courses on this piece of "old California," but there was a conflict of interest between the ranch and the government. Vandenberg Air Force Base objected to increasing the density of the area because of their missile launches. On September 30, 1992, however, the Air Force acquired development rights on the ranch for $22.1 million. Bixby still owned the land, but only thirty-eight homes could be built in designated areas, and no commercial ventures were allowed. The agreement, however, ran against the California Coastal Commission's efforts to secure public access to this section of coast.

156

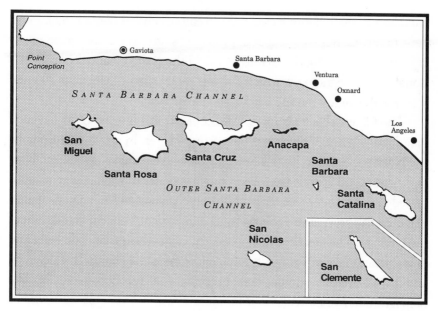

THE CHANNEL ISLANDS

The Channel Islands

Among the Gaviota Land's other important neighbors, the Channel Islands must also be mentioned, if only briefly. There would not be a channel if they did not exist, and Gaviota would be a different land. From the west, these eight islands are San Miguel, Santa Rosa, Santa Cruz, Anacapa, Santa Barbara, San Nicolas, Santa Catalina, and San Clemente. The first four have been referred to by boaters as the "fearsome foursome," as many vessel accidents have occurred around them. The approximate sizes in acres are: Santa Cruz, 60,740; Santa Rosa, 52,758; Santa Catalina, 48,438; San Clemente, 31,500; San Nicolas, 13,370; San Miguel, 9,122; Anacapa, 737; and the smallest, Santa Barbara, 640. Although ocean mists and fogs often prevent their visibility, on a clear day their silhouettes rise up sharply out of the sea across from the Gaviota Land.

The islands have been a prominent part of history in the area and were used by the Chumash, fur traders, and smugglers. President Franklin Roosevelt gave them National Monument status in 1938, and since 1980, five have became the Channel Island National Park (Anacapa, Santa Barbara, San Miguel, Santa Rosa, and the eastern end of Santa Cruz). President Jimmy Carter gave a special protected status to the six square nautical miles surrounding the islands by establishing the Channel Islands National Marine Sanctuary, which shelters thousands of marine species and is one of the largest marine sanctuaries in the world.

The Channel Islands have a direct geological bearing on the coastal mainland. Gaviota's neighbors are getting nearer. In a five-year study by the National Science Foundation, scientists have found that Santa Rosa and Santa Cruz islands have been moving closer to the coast at an estimated rate of one centimeter per year, which causes two meters of slippage of the earth's crust in the channel and is important from the standpoint of earthquakes. The greater the slippage, the larger the quake. The epicenter of the great quake of 1812 was estimated to lie in the channel off Gaviota, and it is felt that the present rate of slippage could produce an earthquake of magnitude 7 or more.

Santa Cruz (Holy Cross) Island, the largest of the chain, is approximately twenty-two miles long, with sixty-five miles of shoreline. It was named when the ship *San Antonio*, under the command of Juan Perez of Portolá's expedition, lost its bearings and landed on the island; the padres forgot a small iron cross, and natives made a long trip in order to return it to them. There are two rugged mountain ranges on Santa Cruz, which enclose a nice valley containing some rare plant species. Justinian Caire bought the island in 1869 and built a Mediterranean-style village, which included a main ranch house (considered elegant), bunkhouses, stables, a winery (which produced some prize-winning vintages), a bakery, and a chapel. Many of these buildings were decorated with ornate ironwork. Edwin Stanton purchased most of the island in 1937, and for years it was a cattle ranch. The Nature Conservancy, a non-profit organization dedicated to saving wilderness areas, acquired control of Santa Cruz Island in 1978, but the descendants of Justinian Caire, the Gherini family, retained the east end of the island, which will be part of the national park. $14.5 million was in President George Bush's proposed budget for acquisition of the sheep ranch.

Santa Rosa Island is the second largest island, about fifteen miles long. It has a variety of plant and animal life, including rare ironwood trees. The remains of a dwarf mammoth were discovered on the island, and it is thought that this animal may have been killed by hunters who lived there 30,000 years ago. In the early years of European settlement, cattle were raised on Santa Rosa. It later became a sheep ranch, and in 1902 Walter Vail and J. V. Vickers bought the island to bring back cattle. For many years thereafter, cattle were rounded up and shipped across the channel, more than 100 head per delivery, many of them swimming in to Gaviota Beach. The National Park Service purchased the land in 1987 for $29.5 million. There are also radar and aircraft controls on the island.

Santa Rosa Island, viewed from Gaviota.

The shortest distance to San Miguel is by boat from Gaviota. This island is about eight miles long and more than four across at its widest. Robert Brooks leased the island for a sheep range in 1928, and Herbert Lester and his wife, Elizabeth (née Sherman), came there to manage it. They were dubbed King and Queen of San Miguel. Their life was similar to Robinson Crusoe's experience on a desert island, except that supplies came once a month by boat, and twice a year a ten-man crew arrived to shear the sheep. The movie *Mutiny on the Bounty*, starring Charles Laughton, was made on San Miguel Island. The Navy used the island as a bombing range during World War II, and it is now administered by the National Park Service.

Ocean winds sweep against the western shore of San Miguel with great force, up to 100 miles per hour, and this land faces the full thrust of the Pacific Ocean. It is famous for its seal and sea lion breeding grounds, where every year from 20,000 to 30,000 pinnipeds congregate to bear young. It is also known for its caliche forest of brittle, fossilized trees preserved in white calcium carbonate. It is believed that Cabrillo used Cuyler's Harbor on the island for an anchorage and that he was buried on San Miguel; a monument to him was erected there in 1936.

Anacapa Island is really three small islands linked by reefs that are above water at low tide, and the three masses of volcanic rock together are about four and a half miles long, with a maximum width of about half a mile. The mirage phenomenon of the channel seems to transform its high cliffs into low flatlands and sometimes appears to erase the land altogether. The isle is considered the "guardian of the channel" with its fog horn and eighty-five-foot lighthouse. It also has a gigantic arched rock at the eastern end and is honeycombed with obscure caves in the steep, wind-eroded cliffs. The middle and western sections are closed to human visitors, as they are the breeding and nesting site of the brown pelican.

The other four islands, Santa Barbara, San Nicolas, Santa Catalina, and San Clemente, are more distant from Gaviota, and although they have contributed much to the natural and political histories of the Channel Islands, they have not been as important as the "fearsome foursome" in the story of the Gaviota Land.

CHAPTER 12
The Beach Area

Alcatraz Landing

Alcatraz Landing was east of the beach in the Gaviota Land. The Alcatraz Company purchased 127.39 acres of land from Hollister on May 17, 1897, to mine Sisquoc asphaltum about thirty miles to the north and pipe it to Alcatraz for refining. Approximately thirty-seven miles of pipeline for two lines were laid from Sisquoc through the Santa Ynez Valley and Gaviota Pass to the landing. Asphaltum had to be mixed with naphtha to maintain liquidity, otherwise it plugged the pipelines; therefore, a four-inch pipe conveyed the liquid asphaltum and naphtha downhill to the refinery, and the two-inch one returned the naphtha to Sisquoc.

On August 16, 1897, the Alcatraz Company was granted a franchise to construct a wharf and to collect tolls for twenty years. The refinery started up the next year, and the endeavor was reported to have cost $1 million. William H. Crocker, of the San Francisco banking family, was a financial backer of the Alcatraz project. William Cowles was its president, and Arthur Bell was in charge of construction. The industry was considered by the Santa Barbara Chamber of Commerce then to be "the only plant of its kind in the world." About fifty men were employed at Alcatraz and seventy at Sisquoc, and the refinery even had its own post office, "Asphaltea," from 1889 to 1901, when it was transferred to Gaviota. The Alcatraz School was established for the children on April 5, 1899. It was a typical little red school house, and a few children even arrived by passenger train from Point Conception.

There was not enough profit from the industry, however, and the com-

Alcatraz wharf.

Logo and postmark of the Alcatraz Company.

Alcatraz School, established 1899.

The Alcatraz Pacific Oil Transportation Co. plant.

Tidewater Associated Oil Company refinery at Alcatraz.

pany began to default on loans in January 1902. By then, cheaper and better deposits of asphaltum had been located at Carpinteria and Goleta. Refinery operations were abandoned and pipelines removed. New lines were laid, however, to carry crude from the Western Union Oil Company's field near Los Alamos to Gaviota. The Pacific Oil Transportation Company operated the refinery.

Ownership of Alcatraz Landing legally changed on May 3, 1904, when the Mercantile Trust Company won a foreclosure suit, and possessions were auctioned off. The property was sold to the Associated Oil Company on June 24, 1905, and they also acquired the pier franchise. Pacific Oil Transportation stock also went to Associated Oil, which merged

The Alcatraz complex included onshore housing and offshore moorings.

with the Tidewater Oil Company on November 30, 1936, to become
Tidewater Associated Oil Company, and crude was tankered to their San
Francisco refinery. A marine terminal with underground pipelines re-
placed the old pier, which was torn down. In 1967, Tidewater merged with
Getty Oil Company, and Texaco took charge of the operations in 1983.

Tidewater's operation at Gaviota was known as the "oil town near the
ocean." To local people, it was the "tank farm." The refinery was close to

The Alcatraz pier accommodated locals as well as oilmen.

the ocean, almost opposite the old Gaviota Store. There were also about ten homes and a boarding house on the east side of Alcatraz Creek on the bluff, and other buildings were across the road. George Thorpe was one superintendent of the Tidewater operation, and Luis Lingchow was a caretaker. In 1900, twenty-seven men listed Alcatraz Landing as their place of residence. The name of Alcatraz was diminishing by 1914, however, as the thirty-five people registered at the Alcatraz precinct all claimed Gaviota as their residence.

The pier at Alcatraz had been built to accommodate oil tankers, but it was also used by individuals for fishing and other recreational pursuits. Joe "Foster" Faustine was one "old timer" who fished and set out lobster traps. Tony Cabral lived in a little house in the canyon and kept a small boat tied to the pier, selling fresh fish to Santa Barbara outlets and drying other quantities. Although the pier didn't have railings, the large cracks in it permitted safe fishing for young children. Tony often went under the pier in his boat to retrieve a catch too large to fit through the cracks, and he was sometimes given wine in appreciation. Julio Greco also had a fishing vessel off Alcatraz, but he drowned while getting lobsters, and it was two weeks before his body was found.

The Rosecrans. There have been many shipwrecks and accidents off the coast. Two were at Alcatraz, and both involved the same ship. The *Rosecrans* was moored to take on a cargo of oil in March 1912, but high waves off the Gaviota Land caused a rope to break, and the Associated Oil Company vessel was driven ashore. Two men drowned while trying to escape in life boats, but the other crew members reached shore by lines. After three tugs, the *Sea Rover*, the *Navigator*, and the *Defiance*, pumped water from the ship, holes were patched, and the vessel was sent to San Francisco for repairs. A second oil boat, the *Falls of Clyde*, escaped damage.

The *Rosecrans* was a smoldering mass about fifty yards offshore at Alcatraz in August of the same year. A series of explosions in the fuel room ripped the boat apart, and flames engulfed it. The cause of the explosions was not known, but at the time the ship had about a thousand barrels of oil on board. The *Rosecrans* was cut loose, and Captain L.F. Johnson and crew watched from the beach as it burned down to the water. It seemed that the vessel had an Alcatraz "hoodoo" after it had been beached and severely damaged there before. It was thought that the vessel would have to be blown up and totally destroyed so as to not obstruct shipping, but the hull was able to be towed to San Francisco for salvage.

Vessels could bring in other things as they were taking on oil, and an unwanted stowaway, the dreaded Mediterranean fruit fly, obtained entrance into California from fruit landed at Alcatraz by ships from Honolulu in 1911. Thereafter, a strict inspection of all vessels would be made.

Vista del Mar School, built in 1927.

Vista del Mar School

The Alcatraz, Las Cruces, and Orella schools combined in 1926 to form the Vista Del Mar (view of the sea) Union School District, and San Julian joined the district around 1950. Until the construction of permanent facilities was completed, classes were held in a two-room structure donated by Tidewater, located near some homes across the road from the Alcatraz School. (The site was later replaced with a large, high fill for the Chevron refinery.) Grades 1-4 were in front; 5-8 were in back. They were separated by a partition, which was sometimes removed for dances. Some of the first teachers were Margret McTavish (grades 1-4) and Margaret Wood (principal and grades 5-8). There were about forty students from Las Cruces to El Capitan who were picked up in an old Model T bus.

The larger, "permanent" two-room school with Spanish architecture and a red-tile roof was built in the Gaviota Land east of the store in 1927 by Hans Skytt of Solvang. A large auditorium seating 250, a bus garage, and a caretaker's house were also part of the complex. A two-room wing and a cafeteria were added later. Behind the school was a uniquely shaped hole in the cliffs which resembled the shape of a rooster. It was the children's "chicken cave."

Laura Gann was an early principal, and Claude Norcross was the first male administrator. At one time, Pince Russell and her husband had

167

The "chicken cave" near Vista del Mar School.

charge of the cafeteria, and June Fitzgerald (née Daudert) and her mother, Rose Hunt, were other chefs. A single custodian initially cared for the yards, cleaned the school, and drove the bus, but later it became necessary to have two. Albert Meloling was one early driver. At one time, Bud Harwood was the driver going east, while Vic Larsen traveled west. Later there were three buses, one of them a van that picked up the children on

Teacher Carolyn Donahue Henning and the class of '41.

A Marine helicopter makes a special delivery to Vista del Mar.

the Hollister Ranch. While living at Gaviota, John S. "Mac" McDonell drove that route. When the San Julian School closed, students from that district were driven to Walter Nielsen's home to meet the big yellow bus. For a while, Mary Minetti made the round trip twide a day in her station wagon.

An F-86 Sabre jet fighter was a special part of the school's playground, arriving just before Christmas in 1959. The principal, Warren Binzley, made an inquiry to General David Wade, commander of the First Missile Division at Vandenberg Air Force Base. Such craft were available, but a veterans' group was needed as a sponsor. The Goleta Amvets Post No. 55 supported the project, and a fighter was located in a depot for outmoded aircraft in Tucson. Vandenberg did not have a helicopter large enough to fly the 6,800-pound plane to the school, but the Marine Helicopter Transport Squadron from the Marine air facility at El Toro volunteered a twin-engine aircraft, and the jet was delivered—half at a time. It was a demilitarized real Air Force jet, complete with cockpit, controls, and instruments, but it did not have an engine, guns, rockets, or bombs.

The jet was placed in the center of the playground and assembled by

Air Force crews flown in by another whirlybird. The entire student body watched its arrival—a joint venture of the U.S. Air Force, Navy, and Marines. The plane had been built eight years earlier at a cost of more than $500,000, but for the next twenty-five years it would be part of playground equipment. Steps were built up after one child fell and broke an arm. Locks also had to be put on it after parts were stolen. The plane was visible from Highway 101, and more than one car stopped to investigate a possible plane crash.

When the school was later forced to move because of the Chevron refinery, the fighter was repossessed by the Air National Guard. It was restored and placed on display at McLennan Air Force Base near Sacramento with a sign about its history.

Smuggling and Prohibition

The remote, isolated shore and rugged cliffs of the Gaviota (Alcatraz) area made a good smuggling site. The Volstead Act of 1920 forbade the sale of alcoholic beverages, and consequently thousands of barrels of bootleg liquor were smuggled into California for distribution to prime markets. It was very difficult for law enforcement to patrol the many miles of coastline, but the Gaviota region was one of the spots where active surveillance was maintained as much as possible. The Lompoc *Record* reported in October 1925 that Sheriff James Ross and his deputies had seized three cars and forty cases of Canadian liquor in a canyon near Gaviota. The liquor bottles, hidden in brush alongside the highway, were still wet from their beach landing. The smugglers escaped, however.

In the dark of the night, rum boats anchored as close to the Gaviota Land as possible. Their arrival was announced by flashing lights from the sea, and accomplices on land waited for the transfer. Some of the vessels were disguised as fishing boats, with fish piled on top of false bottoms. Smaller launches frequently made beach deliveries, but sometimes boats went out through the surf to meet the liquor carrier. It was said that a Gaviota resident drove horses and a wagon out to retrieve the clandestine cargo.

Once ashore, the booze was quickly hidden, often in sheds or storage areas of local residences, and large payoffs were made for permission to do this. Frequently the contraband went underneath a pile of firewood or beneath a hay stack. Usually it was transferred out of the area at night in a variety of vehicles through a diversity of routes. Prearranged locations were sometimes designated for pickup later. Sometimes whiskey was even left floating in the ocean for retrieval. One old-timer accidentally located such a "collection," and when his last bottle broke, he frantically went out to sea in hopes of finding a second supply.

Stills were known to be operating in the Hollister, Cojo, Jalama, and Las Cruces areas. Booze from Cojo was shipped out on freight trains, and a man on an old white horse reportedly followed the railroad tracks from Jalama to Cojo in order to dispense booze. Several families in Las Cruces were known for bootlegging; one woman was a particularly well-known source, and there were other "blind pigs." Three skilled bootleggers made whiskey up the hill at Charlie's Flat, and it was reported that a certain ice company delivered "more than ice."

The bootlegging of liquor ended with the repeal of Prohibition in 1933, but smuggling continued along the coast in drugs. Marijuana and other narcotics were brought in. The channel was still a prime location because of the many hiding places available and the closeness of a enormous Los Angeles market. The mother ships generally remained outside the limit, using smaller speedboats for distribution. Airplanes sometimes dropped waterproof containers in chosen sea locations for later boat retrieval.

Not all drugs had to be brought in however; some were grown on the land. Marijuana was located in the Hollister area in August 1981, when more than 2,000 plants were confiscated in the Santa Anita Canyon. Value on the streets was considered to be $4 million. After removal by chain saws, it was transported by helicopters to the sheriff's station.

Earthquake of 1925

During the same period in which liquor smuggling took place, a massive earthquake jolted and shook the ground and everything on it. The Santa Barbara Channel area is one of the most seismically active areas in the state, with a complex system of local faults. Slippage along the Mesa Fault was believed to have triggered movement on the Santa Ynez Fault, the major east-west fissure that generated the great quake of 1812.

Most California earthquakes originate ten miles underground, and movement comes from an elastic rebound after a build-up and sudden release of strain. Earth waves from six to twelve inches high are often visible, and a "groan" is produced by the shift of elastic wave energy from the ground to the air. It has been described as a heavy sound, sometimes barely audible, but similar to faraway thunder. Those in the Gaviota Land felt these waves and heard the groan when a major quake shook inhabitants on June 29, 1925. The quake measured 6.3 on the Richter scale, where every increase of one multiplies the ground motion by ten. Damage from quakes of various sizes is summarized as follows: 3.5—slight; 4—moderate; 5—considerable; 6—severe; 7—major with heavy damage; and 8—capable of tremendous damage.

The 1925 quake did indeed do severe damage. Some vibrations occurred in the darkness of early morning on June 29. Farm animals became nervous, and about 6:30 A.M., some inhabitants heard the quake approaching. Soon everyone felt the strong vibrations, and many structures were damaged or destroyed. Most of the business district in Santa Barbara was demolished, and stores and hotels were flattened or extensively damaged. One entire wall of the Hotel California disintegrated, exposing all the rooms. Sheffield Reservoir broke, releasing a massive wall of water. Hundreds of aftershocks followed all week, and many people slept and cooked outside. When new buildings were constructed later, more stringent construction codes were enforced.

There weren't many people in the remote Gaviota Land to record quake damage, but it was reported the railroad depot lost a chimney, and things on shelves were hurled to the ground. People saw "waves" in the terrain. Water spouts were visible in the ocean, and springs in Gaviota Pass bulged with water. Chimneys on Rancho San Julian were lost at roof level. The Las Cruces adobe's fireplace is thought to have been destroyed by the 1925 quake. At Cojo, one spring dried up as the land configuration changed, and the water didn't flow anymore; however, another one substituted for it. Wooden fences shook, and barn boards split from ground motion. The cook screamed as the kitchen coffee pot left the stove and spun to the floor, spilling scalding liquid everywhere.

The Chaves family was living in the Gaviota adobe when the quake struck. Ben and his wife were outside with the animals when the powerful shock hit, and the strong earth movement prevented them from opening the heavy corral gates to get back to the house. The ground rocked, boulders tumbled down the hill, and the animals "went crazy." Their five-year-old daughter, Jinny (Eugenia), in her pajamas, grabbed her baby sister and carried her outside to safety. The entire east wall of the adobe came tumbling down, exposing all three rooms. It resembled the Hotel California in Santa Barbara. After the quake, the family slept in small nearby buildings and cooked outside. They were later able to use the adobe's kitchen, but they moved away not long afterward, and the adobe's remains were subsequently entombed under a large highway construction fill.

Another quake came offshore in 1926, and on November 4, 1927, a major earthquake of magnitude 7.3 was centered off Point Arguello. As a result, it is believed, a seismic sea wave rising to eight feet hit the coast, including Gaviota Beach, and was experienced all the way from San Francisco to San Diego.

The Land as It Was

The Gaviota Land of the 1920s was open hills covered with dense grass and brush, and many rattlesnakes and other wildlife made it their home. Willow trees grew along the creeks, and there was an abundance of mustard and wild flowers. In the spring, lupines, buttercups, poppies, and paint brushes peeked up above wild grass. In this land of the gull, their plaintive cries constantly reverberated over the territory, and giant condors circled over the land.

This largest bird of flight lived in the vast adjacent Los Padres National Forest, a very steep mountainous region with elevations ranging to 9,000 feet and more. The condors' home was the Sisquoc Condor Sanctuary in the large San Rafael Wilderness Area. These giant thirty-pound birds with wingspans of up to ten feet roosted on high trees or cliffs, as their flight takeoff was often unsteady. They were not killers, but fed only on the already-dead flesh of other animals. They paired off as couples for life, and usually only one blue-and-green egg was laid per year. It took condors considerable time to reach maturity, and they did not nest until the

Brown pelican, once endangered, now abundant.

sixth year. Their lifespan could be thirty years but was generally shorter. Fighting for survival, these beautiful fliers, once plentiful over Gaviota and other parts of the western United States, gradually became a rare and en- dangered species.

The few remaining birds in California were taken into "protective custody" in a captive breeding program at the San Diego and Los Angeles zoos in 1987. From twenty-seven birds in captivity, the first condor egg was hatched in March 1988. The chick was named Molloko, an Indian word for the giant species. Progress was slow, but additional birds were conceived, and in October 1991, helicopters flew two condors into the Los Padres National Forest, to be released several months later. There was now hope that sometime in the future, these grand birds would again be seen gracefully soaring over the Gaviota Land.

Brown pelicans are also very conspicuous in the Gaviota Land, as their nesting spot is on the west end of Anacapa Island. This fish-eating bird with a wingspan of over six feet often plunges from great heights to snatch fish from the sea near Gaviota, and its pouch can store up to three gallons of water and fish; food is swallowed as water is squeezed out. The brown pelican was once placed on the state's endangered species list because of fragile shells that cracked before hatching, but now the pelicans have increased in numbers with the banning of DDT.

The monarch butterfly is one of the smallest inhabitants of the Gaviota Land. In winter, usually between October and March, large clusters hang from the eucalyptus trees. This is one of their winter roosting spots before their long spring migration inland. These small butterflies can travel great distances—as much as 4,000 miles. Their brilliant coloration also helps them in doing this: it is a warning that the milkweed in their system is poisonous to birds.

Monarchs mate at the end of winter along the coast and then travel inland, where they lay eggs on milkweed plants before dying. After about five days, a caterpillar appears, which eats constantly in order to molt three or four times as its size increases. It then goes through the chrysalis stage, hanging head-down from a branch, and after changing into a colorful green pupa with spots of shining gold, a beautiful monarch later emerges. Several generations repeat this cycle before the autumn migration back to the coast to escape frigid temperatures, and those making the long flight do so for the first time. They are three generations away from the monarchs that made the inland trip earlier in spring.

The Adobe And Other Early Homes. When Gaviota was part of the Hollister Ranch, there were several buildings in the canyon north of the creek. The Chaves family was the last to live in the old adobe, which was so severely damaged by the earthquake. It was considered to be the former old Gaviota Adobe Inn used during stagecoach and wharfing days, and posts and rings for horses still stood outside. Wooden additions had enlarged the original structure, and there was a kitchen, a spacious dining room, a parlor, and another large room in the center. The adobe had at least four bedrooms, and each had a fireplace for heating. Located between the bedrooms were two or three indoor toilets with high pull-chains alongside their basins. The bath was a galvanized tub in an outside room upstairs. There were different wallpapers, mostly in blues and maroon, and the ceilings were high. Corrals were nearby, and there were two large barns along with quite a few sheds for ranch operations.

Ben Chaves was Hollister's gatekeeper. The dirt road into the ranch was only a one-way path in those days, and people coming or going had to call ahead from either the ranch or the adobe to have the gate opened. The beach was private, but people were allowed entrance through the gate. The Chaves children waited to open it for visitors, especially on Sundays, as they were usually given a tip for doing so. Tony Cabral was another gatekeeper, living in a small house built close to the turnoff to the ranch road. Subsequent guardians were in a trailer or, later, a gatehouse at the top of the hill above the beach.

With the adobe obliterated, the Hollister Estate built another house in Gaviota Canyon for its employee Luis Ochoa. He and his son, Tony, lived there until 1938. The house stood near the existing palm tree to the left of the road going to the beach. The tree was planted by Tony in back of the house. The L-shaped house faced the beach and had two bedrooms, a large kitchen, a living-dining room, a big tack room, and a small bathroom. There was a raised, roofed, wooden porch with a railing along two sides of the house and a garden nearby. A barn and garage (with a raised floor), an outhouse, and a chicken coop were also part of the complex. The house was "wide open" underneath; it was built off the ground on "stilts" for protection from the high waters, as heavy rains could and fre-

High water innundates Gaviota Road.

The Hollister house north of Gaviota Creek.

quently did inundate this part of the Gaviota Land.

Smaller buildings were later combined to provide additional bedrooms for larger families, and the house became U-shaped, with four to six bedrooms. Frank and Catherine Pacheco and four sons were occupants; Arnold (Hollister's Las Cruces foreman) and Della Avila and their eight children were other residents. They had a special rose garden and a cow that the children rode like a horse. Beach visitors often thought that the large house was a motel for overnight accommodations, and the front door had to be kept locked to prevent them from coming in to look for rooms. The Larry Cota family, which included nine children, moved in after the Avilas left and was there from 1961 to 1962. Jack Wade, a later ranch employee, was probably one of the last persons to live north of the creek in Gaviota Canyon. His home had a small bar with about four stools with saddles on them, where friends and other employees stopped after work for a beer or two. After the land came under state ownership, all structures in this part of the Gaviota Land were removed.

Welcome to Gaviota Park!

CHAPTER 13

Gaviota Beach
Belongs to the People

County Ownership

The beach area of the Gaviota Land became public domain in 1926. The original wharf property was approximately 550 by 800 feet. It was conveyed to the Pacific Coast Steamship Company in 1901 and to the Honolulu Consolidated Oil Company in 1915. Santa Barbara County purchased 8.8 acres around the beach for $6,000 in January 1926 to provide a county park, and the Hollister Estate Company let the county take over the narrow, ungraded dirt road to the beach.

The county maintained control under a lease agreement until 1969 but gave up title in 1952-53, when the land was deeded to the state in lieu of matching funds for the purchase of El Capitan Beach. It was "traded in" along with $25,000 and Goleta Beach. The acquisition price of El Capitan was $250,000, and Gaviota was then valued at $75,000. Stated another way, the state allocated $225,000 to procure El Capitan, and the county donated Gaviota and Goleta beaches plus $25,000. El Capitan was immediately managed by the state.

The state also acquired Refugio Beach in 1950 with county and state matching funds. Refugio was purchased for $105,000 from the Rutherford family, who had operated it as a private enterprise with fifty-cent car entrance fees. Camping was available, and there were also small cabins which rented for $2 a night. Refugio management was also under a county lease until 1969.

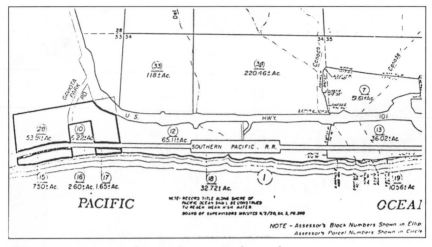

County assessor's map showing Gaviota Park parcel.

Caretaker's cottage at Gaviota Park.

Shortly after the county acquired Gaviota Beach, a two-bedroom caretaker's home was built. Water and outhouses were provided for campers, then restrooms were built along the entry road. As many as 500 people were reported to be at Gaviota Beach on Sundays. At first there was no fee for day use or overnight camping. Later, fifty cents was charged to camp;

Gaviota Beach, circa 1930.

this was increased to $1 for tents and $1.25 for trailers. Tents were pitched on open land, often near the trestle, as it was thought that train clamor helped keep away rattlesnakes. Tents were sometimes tied to cars to hold them up in the notorious winds that could swirl down the canyon. Instead of heading straight out to sea, Gaviota Creek sometimes coiled like a snake through the middle of the beach, and a white raft about twenty feet square was anchored offshore. For those lying on the deck, however, the constant flight of overhead gulls could be a "threat."

County improvements came gradually. A concrete platform was poured in 1931, and a pergola ascended over it the next year. Part of the west hill was torn down in the 1940s, and land was leveled and surfaced for parking. Long and orderly rows of tamarisk trees were planted as wind breaks. The pier and concessions building were constructed in 1951, and the parking lot was paved in 1953. A second facility in the center of the camping area was requested in 1954 (estimated cost $10,000) to provide hot showers, a laundry room, and additional restrooms. Playground equipment appeared in 1955. Twenty-five additional parking spaces south of the trestle, which had been washed away years ago by storms, were finally restored in August 1985, but heavy rains in February 1992 again caused severe damage.

A pergola shades picnic benches at Gaviota Beach.

Hundreds of visitors enjoy Gaviota Beach daily.

Camping at Gaviota Park.

Hank Thygesen with a prize halibut caught off Gaviota Beach. Note the openness of the land and the Hollister Ranch house in the background.

Swimmers enjoy the fresh water of Gaviota Creek as it winds along the beach.

Caretaker Manuel Dutra at work.

Under county management, camping was limited to two weeks in any thirty-day period; day use was between 6 A.M. and dark, and no vehicles were allowed to remain overnight in the parking lot. Sites 1-38 were for recreation vehicles and 41-59 were for tents. No trailers were allowed in the tent areas, and no tents were permitted in trailer spaces. The county also provided an "overflow" area along the east side of the parking lot for travelers unable to get a regular site.

William Hogan, Gates Foss, Manuel Dutra, Carmen Nelson, and their families were some of the caretakers at Gaviota Beach. Resident county rangers later replaced them, and one of the first was "Pinkey" Green. John Van Zander, Bob Jennings, and Roy Champagne were other rangers. Bill Riddle was the last county ranger at Gaviota.

The Pier

The pier at Gaviota is the heart of the area, and the possibility of building such a pier had been discussed years before it was actually built. When the county constructed the overseer's house in 1927, donations of labor and hauling were made for an ocean outlet, but no action was taken. The Lompoc Valley Chamber of Commerce endorsed the pier and agreed to help work out finances. Many individuals had used the Alcatraz pier for fishing and boating, and when the Tidewater Oil Company planned its removal for replacement with two marine loading lines extending out into the ocean, it was hoped that the county could purchase it, but the idea was dropped when repair estimates were greater than the cost of erecting a new structure.

The Lompoc Sportsman Association (and other groups) appeared before the Board of Supervisors in support of the pier, and the county decided to fund the structure. Preliminary figures were ordered, and $50,000 was approved in June 1949. The purchase of Refugio Beach temporarily jeopardized construction, however, as county matching funds were necessary for the state purchase of the beach. It appeared that pier monies might be needed, and the county requested a committee of sportsmen to make recommendations. The pier was favored over the acquisition of additional beach, but eventually both projects were completed.

Although construction had been delayed, plans and specifications

Pilings from the old wharf, foreground, and the new pier, background.

185

The new Gaviota pier.

were drawn in the spring of 1950 for a 540-foot pier. The structure would be 15 feet wide with a 4,500-yard excavation for a vehicle approach, and there would be about 14 feet of water off the end at low tide. There would be a one-ton hoist to launch boats for twenty-five cents. The low bid of $44,482 was submitted by McGray of Santa Maria. (Ralph McGray was one of the early construction contractors who built many of the wharves, piers, and docks between Ventura and San Simeon. He died in February 1992 in Santa Maria at the age of one hundred and one.)

The paths of the past and present crossed during construction, as part of the old shipping wharf was in the way of its replacement. The two angled toward each other. Divers working on the removal of the pier at Alcatraz assisted with the elimination of some of the conflicting segments from the "older brother." Close to the beach at low tide, however, some of the old pilings are still visible, reminders of that past life.

Dedication of the pier, the only boat-launching area in the northern part of the county, took place in April 1951, with the Sportsman Associations in charge. County supervisors were part of a large crowd, and another chapter was written in the history of the Gaviota Land. Ocean access was again available, and it was a vital ocean artery. Along with its ancestor, the old wharf, the modern pier has been vital to the area and a large part of coastal life. The view from the end is a magnificent panorama

Fishing and other activities make the pier the heart of Gaviota life.

of the surrounding terrain and coastline for miles.

The pier was designed for recreational use, but oil companies worked out an agreement with the county to utilize it for transferring personnel and light equipment to their tideland offshore drilling and production operations. Regardless of use, a monthly fee of $250 was charged, plus $2 for each scooter-load of material hauled by county personnel during the day and double fees for night deliveries. No vehicles could be operated on the pier except by a county employee, and the load limit was 1,000 pounds. No company could permit a boat of more than fifty feet to tie up to the pier, and they were responsible for any damages. The money went into a capital outlay fund to be used later for pier improvements. Some of the oil companies involved were Mobil, Phillips Petroleum, Standard, Getty, Shell, and Texaco. Boats frequently docking were *Pat Tide*, *King Tide*, *Run Tide*, *Luck Tide*, and *Pike* X.

Pier Refurbishment and Repairs. The narrow pier required expansion, as only one-way boat travel was possible. Bids were opened in 1964 to widen it seven feet and extend it another thirty feet. The structure would then be twenty-two feet wide and five hundred seventy feet long.

Thaxton Construction Company of Oxnard offered the low bid of $57,480 in October 1966. The county's general fund was not used; rather, $35,000 in pier monies was made available from oil companies, $12,480 from the county's fish and game account, and $10,000 from the tidelands oil royalty fund from state oil leases opposite the county park. The pier was closed in November and reopened in February 1967.

Supplementary launch facilities were also desired at Gaviota. If boats could not get in there, an additional "running time" of about an hour and a half was required to reach Goleta, and two hours for Santa Barbara. Going in the other direction to Avila was almost impossible

The Gaviota pier is widened and extended in 1966–67.

because of having to go "uphill" against rough waves, and towing for disabled boats in either direction took hours longer. During improvement discussions, a second hoist was proposed, but it was not included in final plans.

In order to build a second launch facility, it was suggested in 1967 to raise the twenty-five-cent hoist fee so that money would be available. Since the state was going to take over the operation of Gaviota in 1969, however, the county would not be able to recover the investment, and this idea had to be dropped. In 1983, private individuals, the Lompoc Dive Club, replaced the one-ton hoist with a three-ton unit to allow

The Gaviota pier is pounded by storms and high waves.

ocean access for larger boats, but there were malfunctioning and operational problems which first had to be resolved.

Piers are always subject to damage from the ocean and storms, and the one at Gaviota is no exception. Waves have sprayed over the end in big storms, and water has been ejected up through the cracks like multiple geysers. Closures and repairs have often been required. When high seas damaged many coastal piers in January 1953, they ripped off the boat ladder, landing, and equipment box at Gaviota. (Towering waves also came up as far as the picnic pergola, but chains moored the tables.) Repairs included revising the landing, installing additional pilings, and making modifications to allow the docking of fifty-foot boats.

Closure was required in 1963 for the installation of additional dolphins (piling clusters for boat fenders), and other worn pilings were reconditioned in October 1975. Intense storms damaged and tore up the pier's underside in May 1980, resulting in closure, and during immense squalls, the entire end railing was removed by violent waters. The winter

Repair of boat launching facilities on Gaviota pier.

storms of 1982-3 put the pier out of operation for six months while piling restorations were made by the Associated Pacific Construction Company of Morro Bay; federal and state funds of $74,565 financed the project. Other shutdowns for similar repairs came in October 1985 and August 1987.

Cushman Contracting Company of Santa Barbara had a $110,300 contract in February 1987 for re-decking the pier. In December of that year, a severe storm howled through and wiped out the entire underneath section along with more than fifteen pilings and dolphins which had guarded it. About eight months were necessary for restoration, and fishermen, divers, and boaters were very upset. Work was in the completion stage when a non-union contract resulted in sabotage by union workers. The custom-designed metal steps and replacements were tossed into the massive, moving ocean waters, and it was feared that the specially-designed equipment would be lost forever in the sea currents. After days of extensive diving, however, they were retrieved. It was July 30, 1988, when the pier was finally reopened for boat launching.

In September 1992 a three-inch pipeline was installed under the length of the pier to provide fire-fighting foam to boats combating oil fires at sea. The foam would be trucked to the pier, and the project was funded by Texaco, who would replace the underneath ramp in return, at an estimated cost of $9000. Its slippery, sharp incline had caused many problems.

The Concession and McDonell

At the same time the pier was constructed, the concession at Gaviota was born. The first concessionaires were John S. "Mac" McDonell and Pierce Samuelson, his brother-in-law; together they had previously managed a sporting goods store in Santa Maria. McDonell was on a beach picnic during pier construction and decided to investigate the possibility of a concession. He obtained county permission to build a temporary two-room structure for summer operations, and a contract was approved for operation with 5 percent of gross receipts and 10 percent of rentals to go to

John S. "Mac" McDonell, Gaviota concessionaire 1952–1972.

John McDonell's little red house at Gaviota.

the county. The summers were profitable, and McDonell and his wife, Edythe (Ede), relinquished their Santa Maria interest and moved permanently to Gaviota, where they were concessionaires for many years.

McDonell also obtained county approval to build a rent- and tax-free "little red house" adjacent to the caretaker's home. During construction, the family lived temporarily in a large tent which had a wooden floor, space for four beds, and a clothes dresser. The structure was later converted into a garage. The temporary concession was taken down, to become part of a house bedroom, and the county built a permanent concession and restrooms on the former site. C. V. Nielson of Solvang was the successful bidder at $7,421. McDonell later rented the house, and when he left it was sold to the state for a ranger's residence. It was then occupied by other park personnel. Alison Strachen (née Odum) was there for a long time.

The concessionaire initially collected the camping fees at the beach and received a percentage of the money collected. To avoid expenditures for updating existing structures, required under state housing regulations, the county assumed this responsibility in 1955, as county operations did not come under these requirements. Concession items were sold through a large outside window, and there was no customer entrance into the store. McDonell had wood, ice, butane, a few groceries, nonalcoholic drinks, fishing equipment (including licenses), juicy hamburgers, and freshly-made popcorn and milkshakes. There were also about ten fourteen-foot wooden boats, which rented for $15 a day.

Ed Hauenstein had the early boat franchise at Gaviota for both charter and public use. He operated the *Lorayne* to the Channel Islands, leaving the pier at 7 A.M. and returning at about 4 P.M., which allowed approximately five hours for catching the "big ones." McDonell later had the contract. Alexander Bradley had approval in 1967 for a boating franchise off Gaviota.

McDonell was the longest concessionaire at the beach—his tenure lasted twenty years. Others had it for shorter periods, and business became a walk-in service. McDonell left in 1972, a few years after state management came in, and Lou and John Davis operated the franchise. Bruce Nix took over for a few years in July 1979, and Bob Parker was there from July 1981 until 1984. Ed Grossi followed him until October 1989, and Parker reassumed management from December 1989 to September 1992.

The Rescue. McDonell was involved in a rescue mission in 1953, and he himself had to be saved. A boat belonging to Worth Lundin drifted out to sea, and McDonell left in one of his small skiffs to get it. The motor was not powerful enough, however, for the forceful offshore winds and choppy water, which were carrying him out to sea. He tried to row back far enough to reach a Getty Oil terminal, and there was panic when he missed it. He was able, however, to snag the last terminal and waved his T-shirt as a distress signal. It was after dark when the Coast Guard got to him, and the family lit a fire on the beach to help direct the rescue. McDonell was taken to Santa Barbara, where reporters took pictures and interviewed the "good Samaritan" who had tried to save a boat but had to be rescued himself. It was the top story on the front page of the Santa Barbara *News-Press* the next day, April 10, 1953 (with an erroneous headline). The lost boat was history.

Area newspapers noted McDonell's rescue.

The County Loses Control of Gaviota Beach

There were citizen concerns over state control of both Gaviota and Refugio beaches, and in 1965 petitions were signed to return these parks to the county. There was apprehension that if the state took over the operation, a day-use fee would be charged. It was! Improvements and repairs were needed, and the county hesitated to spend large sums of money on property it did not own. The county hoped to reacquire title from the state, and if this was not possible, a fifty-year lease, since there was no option for renewal when the present agreement expired in 1969.

The county even considered a premature cancellation of its lease in 1967 to allow the state to have earlier control so that needed improvements could be made, but the state was reluctant because of financial difficulties in Sacramento. The state Department of Parks and Recreation had been required to cut its budget by 10 percent and wanted the county to continue management until the end of the lease. County park commissioners agreed that the parks should remain open, voting to continue operating them even though it cost them $20,000 annually. The state took over Gaviota in April 1969.

CHAPTER 14

Gaviota State Park

State Management

When the state acquired additional land to expand Gaviota, it killed the county's hope of reacquiring title to the beach. The voters approved a park bond fund of $150 million in November 1964, and the state purchased several thousand acres around Gaviota at a cost of $2,617,880. The land included additional shoreline from west of the beach to east of Arroyo Hondo, increasing the coastal expanse from 550 to around 27,000 feet. It also encompassed the historic Gaviota Pass and a large part of the Las Cruces area, including the hot springs, which now became part of the Gaviota Land.

Also included in the land purchases were eighty-two acres surrounding the original wharf property, which contained two thousand feet of ocean frontage. The state obtained a deed from the Hollister Company for an undivided one-half interest of this property in October 1967 and exercised eminent domain to acquire the remaining one-half interest from the Dibblee Estate Company and individual family members, who were awarded $148,532 in 1969.

As a result of the additional land, the Gaviota-Hollister boundary was changed, and the ranch guardhouse at the top of the west bluff was moved much further west. Gaviota was classified as a state park, and the former Gaviota of 8.8 acres now encompassed more than 2,700 acres. Gaviota's name took precedence over others and became the district appellation— California Department of Parks and Recreation, Gaviota District—which included Gaviota State Park, Refugio State Beach, El Capitan State

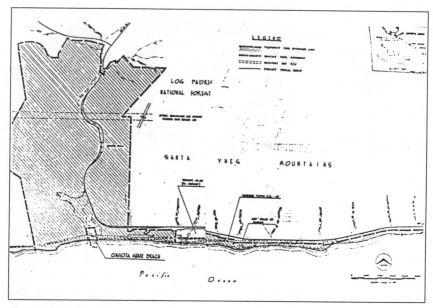

California Department of Parks and Recreation map of Gaviota State Beach.

Beach, Chumash Painted Cave, and El Presidio de Santa Barbara. La Purísima Mission was a satellite.

There were some unsure boundary lines and controversy over cattle trespasses between the state and the Hollister and Pedotti ranches for a while. The cattle did not know that ownership had changed, and they continued to wander onto state property to graze as they had done in the past, but after discussions and negotiations, new fences were finally installed and conflicts were resolved.

Along with recreational use, the state initially continued the county's policy of allowing oil companies to use the Gaviota pier for personnel and supplies. In summer, the companies could use the pier at night after 7 P.M., but in daytime they could only operate on it for personnel between 11 A.M. and 1 P.M. While recreational use was to have priority, complaints were made that oil company operations were in violation of regulations against commercial and industrial activity within a public recreational area. Oil vessels sometimes delayed the launching and hoisting of boats and caused snarling of fishing lines around pilings, in addition to loud noise.

Not long after the state took over Gaviota Beach, a day-use fee was initiated. It increased from $1 to $1.50 in 1976, and overnight camping rates went from $3 to $4. The day charge was $3 in 1982, and camping was $6. Day costs rose to $4 in 1987, and camping charges increased from $8 to $12. Renewed state budget problems in Sacramento in September 1990 caused day-use fees to rise to $6. Camping rates rose to $14, and $16 would be charged from Memorial Day to Labor Day. Extra-car charges increased from $4 to $6, and annual day-use passes sprinted from $50 to $75—a 50 percent increase. Boat hoist fees jumped from $2 to $5, and even per-person charges were considered. There were cries that the state was taking advantage of its unique resources and trying to balance its budget at the expense of campers. The state was the guardian of beaches and parks for all the people, but such high costs might prohibit the public from enjoying them.

In July 1982, Gaviota was one of nineteen parks that the state had scheduled for closure from October to April. This was a money-saving measure; $3.5 million had been cut in the park budget. When they were to be reopened, regular fees were to be increased, and new charges were to be imposed for previously free services. There was great local public uproar, however, and the closure decision for Gaviota (and Refugio) was rescinded, attributed to an "error in staff judgment."

In addition to greatly increasing costs, the state began putting its parks on a reservation system, and Gaviota was the last beach to remain on the first-come, first-served basis. The reservation system had been inaugurated for Hearst Castle, but one by one, other parks were included. State coffers had an appetite for the millions of dollars from the lucrative program. Ticketron held the contract for many years, but an agreement was made in 1986 with a new company, MISTIX, even though it was one of the highest bidders. Competitors contended that false financial data had been submitted, and there was more than one hearing on this decision.

Many people did not like the reservation system. Reservation charges elevated already high camping fees. Travelers often did not have any place to stay if they had not been able to make arrangements months ahead. For those who did, plans often changed, and cancellations had to be made—at additional cost. An unclaimed reservation could not be given

Gaviota park still 'reservations only'

By Richard Aguirre
News-Press Staff Writer

State officials will continue a controversial "reservation-only" policy for allocating campsites at crowded Gaviota State Park despite complaints about it by area residents and state Sen. Gary Hart.

William S. Briner, director of the state Parks and Recreation Department, told the News-Press that the reservation-only system is more effective than the old "first-come, first-served" system replaced in March.

In August, the county Board of Supervisors unanimously recommended that the state set aside half of the campsites at Gaviota for first-come, first-served usage.

Hart, D-Santa Barbara-Ventura, asked for a return to that system during a meeting with Briner in Sacramento last week, but said the request was rejected.

"For the time being, it (Gaviota) is going to remain in the reservation system," Briner said. "It is not my intention to go back to the old system."

While acknowledging local complaints about the new system, Briner said he must try to ensure that all state residents have access to the 70 campsites at the popular South Coast facility

"The parks belong to all of the people," Briner said. "We have to consider first the statewide interest of any unit. We believe all of our units have statewide significance."

However, Hart said that he will seek at least a partial return to the first-come, first-served system when the Legislature reconvenes in December.

"A reservation system for state parks is probably a good idea, but that doesn't mean that all of our parks should be reservation-only," Hart said. "Those of us who are more spontaneous in our vacation plans deserve a chance to enjoy at least some of our state parks."

All campsite requests at Gaviota — and nearly all other state parks — have been handled since March by the MISTIX telephone reservation system.

See Page C-4, Col. 1

State will continue policy on reservations

Continued from Page C-1

which is operated on a contract basis by a private firm.

California and out-of-state residents call in camping reservations to state parks by using a toll-free number. If a desired campground is full, operators can book a reservation at an available facility.

After a wave of local protests — and at Hart's request — state officials agreed that Gaviota would be switched to the reservation system on a "trial" basis for the first year and then undergo a review.

But Hart said local residents want a return to the old system now. They contend they are being denied access to Gaviota and have also complained that:

—Some campers make multiple reservations or don't show up after reserving a campsite, so local residents are turned away while campsites sit empty.

—The system is unfair to those who because of jobs or other reasons cannot make reservations months in advance.

—Those without credit cards cannot use the reservation system.

—There are an inadequate number of reservation telephone lines.

—Under the reservation system, campsite fees have been raised.

In response, Briner admitted that fees were increased, but he disputed the other allegations and said that the MISTIX system has been a success.

Empty campsites have always been a problem, but Briner said that campsites are not sitting empty for consecutive days. If a potential camper — who has already paid up for the first night — doesn't show up, the campsite becomes available.

Briner said that reservations can be made only two months in advance and reservations are accepted from people without credit cards.

While conceding that the MISTIX line was jammed earlier in the summer, he said that additional telephone lines have been added and that other problems are being ironed out.

"This is the first time that any telephone system of this magnitude has been put into place," Briner said. "Everybody underestimated the numbers of people who would call."

Briner said he welcomes legislative or public review of MISTIX, but cautioned that campsites at Gaviota would remain in demand regardless of the reservation system.

"By any system, it (Gaviota) will be full during the summer," Briner said. "Gaviota is very popular."

Fees and reservations caused an uproar at Gaviota State Park.

to another user, and so fewer people were actually using park facilities. While campers were vying for reservations, some sites actually sat empty.

Although Gaviota was the last state beach *not* on the system, it too was added in 1986, but only on a one-year trial basis. Editorials and articles were written in newspapers, and thousands of signatures went to Sacramento for reversal of this decision. Many people wanted the majority of parks returned to the first-come, first-served basis. The Santa Barbara County Board of Supervisors voted unanimously to request that at least half of Gaviota's sites be returned to the former procedure. Gaviota was, consequently, taken off the reservation system, but the state may try to reinstate it into the profitable computerized program.

Resident state rangers were Dave Felt, Mark Windham, Vic Graves, Ted Jackson, Dave Silver, Robin Dressler, and Steve Jones. After Jones left, ranger supervision at Gaviota was periodic surveillance by automobile, and local attention was from camp hosts, who lived rent-free in their

Editorial cartoons criticized state management of Gaviota Beach.

recreational vehicles with some utilities provided. Some of Gaviota's camp hosts have been Bob and Maryl Utter, Bob Hartley, Lou and Lil LaPoint, Wilbur "Bill" Katin, John Gorham, and Jack and Jean Della Santa.

Plans. In 1969, the state planned for two-stage improvements at Gaviota. Preliminary arrangements were for a camp area in the uplands about three miles from the beach. Expenditures in the first five years were estimated to be $3.4 million, and more than $17 million was calculated for the second fifteen-year period. Ultimate development was to include 1,070 picnic units, 1,186 family camp sites, 144 group areas, and parking for 3,750 day-use vehicles, in addition to trails and improvements in the Las Cruces area, but these plans were never executed.

Gaviota Beach was again tentatively scheduled for development in 1979, using funds from the 1974 Park Bond Act. A sanitation station, eleven campsites, forty picnic tables, and fifty-five parking spaces would be added. Two new restroom facilities would also be constructed. It was also proposed that a train stop be considered at the Gaviota siding. The historic buildings at Las Cruces would also be restored, and additional parking, restrooms, picnic tables, walk-in campgrounds, and trails to other park regions would be built. But these conceptions were also only ambitions. The blueprints were made, but the "builder" did not start the job.

Funds were again earmarked for rehabilitation in the Gaviota Land in 1984/85, 1985/86 and in 1989/90, but nothing was done. Major improvements were made at the sister beaches of Refugio and El Capitan, and numerous bond funds were designated for work at Gaviota, but conditions didn't change, and age was showing. Many felt that Gaviota was like Cinderella—her two stepsisters got all the new clothes.

The California Department of Fish and Game requested county funds in the fall of 1990 to modify the fish barrier in Gaviota Creek, which prevented steelhead trout from reaching spawning and rearing habitats. The cost was estimated to be $50,000, which would come from the Coastal Resources Enhancement Fund. The project would remove a portion of the existing bridge structure and reconstruct an appropriately sized opening for fish passage with box culverts. This would probably be done in conjunction with other park improvements.

The Gaviota District and the Channel Coast District (the latter encompassing Carpinteria, McGraff, San Buenaventura, and Emma Woods state beaches) were combined in the fall of 1992 in order to consolidate personnel. The landmark Gaviota Beach was again scheduled for a facelift in that year, using 1984 bond appropriations. The $1.8-million project included restoration of wetlands along Gaviota Creek and Lagoon by the U.S. Army Corps of Engineers; 16,650 cubic yards of landfill to be deposited over the old campground, raising its elevation several feet; a new kiosk and concessions building ; new and relocated restrooms; rearrangement of tent and trailer sites into a circular design with tables and fire rings; and a new eighteen-space overflow area for overnight use by nine self-contained vehicles. There would also be new water-supply lines and a 2,400-cubic-foot sewage disposal field, but the existing well would continue to provide water, treated by the existing treatment plant. The two houses would be removed, leaving no permanent residence at the beach.

Other Plans

There were other changes proposed in the Gaviota area which did not come to pass. In the early 1970s, Gaviota was to be the first in a statewide concessionaire program, which would allow investments of private capital in state parks. It was proposed to allow a concessionaire to finance, construct, and operate a camp on 500 acres on the eastern bluff (at an estimated cost of $2 million). The state would be responsible for law enforcement and safety. Plans were for 350 campsites, 30 picnic sites, 400-car parking, a snack bar, a grocery store, laundry facilities, RV sanitation stations, sport-fishing service, and a tackle shop. The beach campsites were to be removed, and picnic sites placed in the parking area. Charles Carmichael and Edward Hauenstein of Lompoc designed plans for the venture, but the project was not attempted. There were concerns about the climate and the well-known winds in the Gaviota Land, but more important was the questioning of the use of private capital in state parks. It was feared that the profit motive could dominate the park system. In the end, it was decided that the project wasn't "feasible" at Gaviota.

The YMCA of metropolitan Los Angeles purchased the largest parcel (160 acres) on the Hollister Ranch to establish a camp for 250 boys. The complex was to include facilities for outdoor recreation, water treatment, a central dining hall, a conference center, and administrative offices. There were concerns about changing the rural atmosphere, about the large numbers of people and activities in a private area, and about encouraging public access through YMCA easements and memberships. After more than a decade of conflict and negotiation, the large section was sold to private interests and had the same status as other parcels.

Another proposal that did not materialize was a national seashore area. This recommendation was made after the state had acquired a portion of the "big ranch." It was considered ideal for a national seashore area to adjoin a state beach park. This would have extended west down the coast to the Southern California Edison Company property. Also mentioned at one time was an underwater recreation area off Gaviota. This would have stretched along 70,000 feet of shoreline and seaward to the kelp bed, totaling about 1,600 acres.

No safe harbor existed between Santa Barbara and Avila, and the channel waters could be treacherous. A harbor was suggested at Cojo Bay, but the plan was dropped when Vandenberg Air Force Base officials felt the location would be in a danger area from missile launches. A proposal of $500,000 for a harbor of refuge near Gaviota was received by the State Small Craft and Harbors Commission in 1966. The U.S. Army Corps of Engineers would develop breakwaters and do dredging, while the state could extend a fifty-year loan for development of the interior facilities. Maintenance and operation could be under a county contract.

201

Unfortunately, the harbor did not come into existence.

The Southern California Edison Company planned an electrical generating plant just east of Point Conception in 1972, and close to the same area, Western Liquid Natural Gas (LNG) Terminal Associates (an affiliate of Pacific Gas and Electric Company) proposed to construct and operate a terminal with associated pipeline facilities at Point Conception in 1981. Liquid gas was to be transported there to be converted into natural gas. Neither plant was ever built.

A $60-million major supply base for offshore oil and gas platforms between Santa Barbara and San Luis Obispo was sought at Cojo (Damsite Canyon) on 100 acres leased from the Bixby Company by Coastal Services. The proposal for warehouses, storage yards, a heliport, rail sidings, a 1,700-foot pier, and office, administrative, cafeteria, and maintenance buildings was withdrawn, however, when the economy indicated that only half the expected platforms were going to be erected.

High Winds and Storms

Hurricane-force gusts, estimated at up to eighty miles per hour, have roared through Gaviota, ripping down tents and bouncing trailers. Chairs and fishing boxes have flown off the pier. Garbage cans have rolled out to the sea if not clutched by chains. Old-timers felt that even a cup of coffee had whitecaps at Gaviota. Trains were held up in August 1956 for such winds; it was considered dangerous for them to cross the trestle. High gales were also on record in April 1988.

Several railroad car tops had been ripped off by these strong air currents. One lay on the beach in 1975 for several days until a truck and crane came to remove it. The side of a box car blew off and lay under the trestle by the concession. In May 1984, the entire container that had been on top of a railroad flatcar was ripped off by the wind, to stay tilted on the same hillside.

Storms have taken a toll on the area, and severe ones have caused closure of the park, as in February 1973. In January and February 1983, a full moon brought the highest tides in many years, and severe weather hit the channel and beaches. Winds and rainfall were high, many roads were closed, and lands were inundated. Another potent tempest arrived in

High winds actually blew railroad cars from the Gaviota trestle.

January 1988; violent surf again pounded the coast, and high tides caused twenty-foot breakers.

Great waves during such storms have washed massive amounts of debris into the parking lot at Gaviota, which has been said to resemble a battlefield. They undermined the large cement platform, cracking, breaking, and tumbling big concrete masses all over the area. Gaviota made the news on Channel 7 (Los Angeles) on February 4, 1987, when small offshore tornadoes were reported by "Dr. George" Fischbeck. One "tornado" struck the beach in February 1992. It could be seen coming off the water. The force overturned a dumpster and lifted a recreational vehicle up and bounced it down again, causing considerable damage. The neighboring motorhome lost all windows on one side as glass crackled and exploded everywhere.

Gaviota Creek becomes a rain-swollen rapid in the pass.

Not all water damage at Gaviota came from high, salty seas, however. The flooding freshwater from Gaviota Creek could also be disastrous. Ferocious rains in February 1992 caused the swollen river to flow through the entire park with waves as it gushed to the sea outside its regular channel. Afterwards, mud and silt coated the land, even venturing into restrooms. Great debris was left on the beach, and the park was not open for camping for over a month.

The surging beach creek at the "bridge" has also carried numerous vehicles into the swirling water. One driver's pickup was buried in the river in December 1991. Eugene Leader tried to ford the massive bridge water on February 15, 1992, and his car somersaulted into the racing current that quickly hurled it downstream. He managed to escape through a window but suffered from hypothermia. He had almost drowned in Gaviota's waters. Tanya Teget and Allida Allen tried to drive their sedan across the creek on March 5, 1992, and they were rolled all the way to the ocean before they were able to get out. They thought they were going to have a burial at sea.

The portion of Gaviota Creek in Las Cruces and the pass has been an

204

Heavy rains swell Gaviota Creek, flooding roads (note car)…

…and inundating the entrance kiosk.

even swifter river. The Humphries family in Las Cruces lost ducks and pheasants one year, and Hollister Ranch lost cattle. They became stranded on islands, and high water took them with it. In the pass, vehicles went fast downhill on the old road with its sharper curves, and numerous cars have spun over into the current; parts were ferried out to sea. One Model A car went into the stream just north of the pass, turning upside down. As the water receded, its wheels were revealed. Close to the same area, a semi-trailer truck also went swimming. The frame was wrapped around a concrete pipeline support belonging to the Associated Oil Company, but the body and motor of the large vehicle were gone! The truck had carried cans of tomatoes, and people from all around tried to retrieve them as they somersaulted over boulders. A rest-area traveler stacked them up as they rolled by. One oil truck flipped over at the pass itself, and more than one produce truck also overturned there. Lettuce, onions, and strawberries have been dumped into the racing water, and people scurried to retrieve anything salvageable.

Gaviota Glimpses
In 1960, an oil company helicopter landed in the Gaviota parking lot to pick up McDonell's daughter, Donna, to take her out so that she could get to school. Jack and Jan Steinmann lived in McDonell's house when water came to their doorway in one storm. Jan and her three young children got out by climbing up to the trestle and crossing it. At another time of storms and high creek waters, campers Mel and Ruth Creps and county ranger Bill Riddle and his wife, Shirley, were isolated at the beach for about ten days, sharing food. Water and sand were three feet over the entrance bridge then, and no one could get in or out. One ranger attempted to get across, but his jeep overturned—another river vehicle casualty.

From the pier, the coast is visible for miles, a truly spectacular sight of nature's splendor, and there aren't many places like this where you could have seen helicopters transporting the president of the United States, Ronald Reagan, to the "California White House" as they circled over the hills and ocean.

Many archeologists and others visit Gaviota to study the tilted strata which resulted from the massive upheavals and land twisting of years ago.

Tilted rock strata at Gaviota Beach reveal the earth's past

Classes are often conducted there. The mouth of Gaviota Creek is also a critical stop-off point for birds migrating along the coast of California, and the area is recognized by birders and ornithologists as a significant site.

Two horses were down on the beach sands in March 1985—an unusual sight. They were accompanied by a beautiful girl in a long dress, which blew gracefully in the wind, as cameras snapped to take pictures for a high school yearbook.

Carl Johnson once stayed in the old Gaviota depot and used to check the status of fishing by flashing a mirror to those on the pier. Waving hands indicated that it was worthwhile to get a pole.

Certain pelicans have become "pets" on the Gaviota pier and have been known to everyone by name. "Henry" was lame and limped as he came up to greet friends. His successor, "Charlie," was everyone's friend when edibles were offered, which was often. Gimpy was another lame totipalmate who made friends on the pier.

Gaviota had a "streaker" in the 1970s. He came down the pier covered only with a towel and started to crawl over the railing, intending to

David Chesnut with an oil company buoy retrieved as it floated by Gaviota pier.

jump. He was detained by fishermen, however, given additional covering, and the sheriff was called to escort the gentleman elsewhere.

On Mother's Day, 1989, a twelve-year-old boy climbed two-thirds of the way up the western sixty-foot Gaviota cliff, where it became too dangerous to go either up or down, He was immobilized on the steep rock mountain until rescuers summoned by the 911 emergency service could get there. One mother will always remember that day!

Fires in July 1981 scorched 100 acres around Gaviota, but there was no structural damage. Traffic on Highway 101 and trains were blocked off from the area for three hours, however, when high winds whipped flames on both sides of the highway near Gaviota Village. Although the oil tanks were threatened, there was no damage. Gaviota Beach was the command center for a fire in May 1984 which closed one lane of Highway 101, but airplanes assisted in smothering the fire by dropping colored chemical extinguishers on it.

Everyone in the Gaviota Land was apprehensive when a large gorilla was reported to be stalking the area. It was wounded, which made it worse. The "gorilla" was found to be a large black bear that had been struck by a car near the Gaviota Store. Its massive paws were outstretched, and when his enormous hairy face stared directly at the frightened driver through the window, he had indeed resembled an angry gorilla, but a wounded bear was bad enough.

The high mineral content of Gaviota water has always been a problem. A 1,200-gallon tank was installed in 1973 for drinking water, and a reverse-osmosis plant replaced it in 1976. It was hoped that this would make potable well-water, but problems continued, and they are still waiting patiently for a solution. The water dilemma forced park closure on one occasion. No one was allowed to come into the park, and visitors already there were requested to leave unless they were completely self-contained. Eventually there was only one family left. Imagine being the only ones camping at the beach—it was an eerie feeling to be alone in an area once bustling with noise and activity. Silence dominated the air, and no sounds were heard except the voices of the sea and an occasional airplane or train. There were no people on the once-crowded beach and pier. It was as if an atomic bomb had hit. (The family was that of the author.)

Gaviota Charlie. Charlie Foode, an Indian from Alaska and one of twelve children, was known as "Gaviota Charlie" or "Eskimo Charlie." He was a part of the pier scene for over thirty years, and everyone knew him. He had numerous stories to tell and many memories of Gaviota. One was of seeing a horse early one morning running all by himself across the trestle of the "iron horse," coming from the east. A train was racing behind him, and the engineer was frantically blowing the whistle. Realizing the threat, the animal started running at a full gallop and resembled a great big dog as he tried to beat the train. This was one worried horse, and everyone watched the outcome, spellbound. He did make it, however, and the train sped past him just after he got off the tracks. The animal was quickly taken into custody.

Gaviota Charlie.

People returning to Gaviota year after year knew Charlie would be there fishing on the pier. He was friendly with everyone, young and old. He could, at times, also be considered Gaviota's Paul Bunyan. He loved to joke and humor tourists with "tall tales." The Channel Islands, for instance, were: "huge rocks sticking up at low tide"; or they really were "the Hawaiian Islands in the distance." Charlie is no longer there, however; he died May 13, 1992.

Movies. The Gaviota area has been the site for various movies. Several days were spent by producers on a wrecked ship off Point Conception. About ten rodeo cowboys herded cattle on Hollister beaches, where people, houses, and telephone poles weren't visible. One helicopter drove the animals, and another filmed the process as directions were given from the beach with walkie-talkies. The bulls were often obstinate. They had ten thousand feet of film to edit down to forty-five feet for a thirty-second

210

Mountain lions are among the residents of the Gaviota Land.

commercial to be shown during prime time and highly rated shows such as the World Series.

Special models have also been flown to the Rancho San Julian for movies, although the location was not identified to respect the privacy of the ranch. At one time, a six-page supplement to the New York *Times* was filmed there in the rolling hills.

Various car and beer commercials have also been made using the pier at Gaviota. Tom Clancy and Russell Mickey were there when *Big Wednesday* was filmed. Those fishing were allowed to remain, although they were requested not to look at the camera. A temporary concession was constructed on the end of the pier.

Lions. Mountain lions continued to roam the Las Cruces hills. Walter Henning had one glaring down at him from a tree by his home near the hot springs in 1987. Bullets were fired, but the lion escaped. Claw marks were also found on the horses, and one vicious cat was apprehended in a wire trap.

A modern lion hunter was needed in Las Cruces in March 1992 when a nine-year-old boy was attacked while hiking with his family. The lion followed them in the back country; there was a rustle in the bushes, and

211

Large bat ray caught by David Chesnut at Gaviota.

the big cat suddenly lunged and knocked down Darron Arroyo, dragging him into the bushes, where it sank in its teeth and clawed the boy's head, neck, face, and back. His father grabbed a large rock and fired it into the animal's skull. The savage beast left, bleeding, and the boy was picked up and driven as quickly as possible to the Lompoc Hospital. He was in surgery for five hours for fifty puncture wounds, and almost lost his left eye. This is thought to be the only known attack in Santa Barbara County, and modern professional trappers and trained hounds searched for the wild animal. The park was closed indefinitely while the hunt continued.

Fish. There is good fishing off the Gaviota Land, and commercial boats come long distances to be there. A large school was off the coast in September 1988 when three spotter planes and twelve boats searched for them; some of the vessels moored overnight at Gaviota. This occurred again in October 1990. Pier piscatorial catches include perch, cod, barracuda, halibut, white sea bass, corbina, and others. During a mackerel "run," five or more thrashing fish are brought over the rails at once; tails flip and flop everywhere. When abundant bonito were caught in earlier years, some were merely stacked in garbage cans for others to take. A fish is not always what is "biting" on the other end of the line, however; poles, reels, chairs, and even a black brassiere and pair of men's jockey shorts (size 34) have been "caught."

Large bat rays also swim in the waters. David Chesnut hooked a 155-pound ray and landed it on the beach. It was returned to the ocean, but if it had been registered, this Gaviota catch would have taken the state trophy for that year. Seals, dolphins, and whales are often visible in the ocean, and it has been said that some whales occasionally come by close enough to use the pier to scrape off barnacles.

Sharks also lurk in the water. A commercial diver off Gaviota had a section of his scalp taken off by one. His head and shoulders were in its massive mouth, and although he managed to escape, he was badly injured. A big blue shark swam close by the pier in the 1960s, and sticking out of its mouth was a smaller three-foot shark. It was big brother's lunch! On August 30, 1992, an eight-foot blue shark was actually gaffed off the pier.

At one time, hundreds of seals were being chased by a pod of hungry orcas near a small boat belonging to Louis Ruiz. There was great thrashing and splashing of water as the seals fought for their lives, and some of the them seemed to beg with their eyes to get into the boat. As the seals continued in flight on down the coast, two large orcas stopped, and a huge eye quietly stared at the boat from each side, as if contemplating a different meal. It was time to get out of there!

A Few Boating Accidents. Small boats have tossed and heaved in the ocean swells off Gaviota, and some of their broken carcasses have washed up on the rocks. There have been numerous boating mishaps in the area; following are some of them.

In November 1959, six young people narrowly escaped drowning when their sixteen-foot boat capsized in choppy seas, and they were in the cold and perilous water for more than three hours before a rescue was made. That would be a long time to worry about hungry "jaws."

Wind currents double the danger. Once, while two men tried to get their boat motor started in an ocean of whitecaps, the offshore wind carried them three or four miles out to the kelp beds. The Coast Guard was called, but the vessel could not be located. A helicopter was sent from Point Arguello, and search operations went up and down the coast for several days. The missing vessel was finally located off Anacapa Island, but the helicopter went down in the rescue, and a large vessel had to be dispatched from Santa Barbara to save it, too.

Some crafts have just disappeared into the ocean. George Smith and Bill Rickmen left Gaviota in a red and white boat with half a tank of gas, never to return. Smith's body was found in Santa Monica waters, but the boat and his companion were never recovered.

Survivors from another missing vessel were landed right on Gaviota Beach by a helicopter. In the 1960s, another whirlybird descended on the end of the pier itself to carry a wounded diver out on a stretcher. There wasn't much space; people had to be roped off, and the chopper narrowly missed hitting a tall light pole on the corner of the pier.

Around 1950, three young soldiers from the Army Disciplinary Barracks near Lompoc (later the Federal Correctional Institution) went out in a borrowed surplus rubber raft (Worth Lunden's) with only paddles. Offshore winds came up and carried them out to sea. The raft turned over three times in the turbulent waters, and three days later a freighter found it upside down fifty miles down the channel and out to sea. Nealy, the only survivor, lay unconscious on top of it. He had tied himself to the raft and later told about the waves, which seemed to him to be "as high as eucalyptus trees." One companion left in the night, and it was not known when the sea had claimed the third man.

Murder Down the Beach. A brutal murder occurred near Gaviota in June 1963. Two Lompoc High School seniors, Robert Domingos and Linda Edwards, were shot on a lonely stretch of beach on "ditch day." They were to have graduated in a couple of days and had planned to be married later in the year. They were both shot numerous times, and their bodies were dragged to a crude lean-to on the beach. It was set on fire to hide the crime, but it failed to burn, and the bodies were discovered the next day. Flags were flown at half mast, and an intensive investigation ensued up and down the state, but the double murder was never solved.

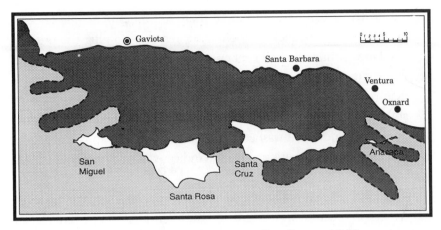

SANTA BARBARA CHANNEL OIL SPILL, 1969

Oil Spill of 1969. The Gaviota Land was part of the biggest oil spill in the channel, which still burns in local memories. Union Oil and its three partners, Texaco, Mobil, and Gulf, had paid $61.4 million for 5,400 acres of oil leases in the channel. The spill was the result of a disastrous eruption of Union Oil's Platform "A," which blew out, sending millions of gallons of

A section of Gaviota Beach after the 1969 oil spill.

crude into the ocean and onto more than 100 miles of shore. The sea turned black with the slick. It took about ten days to plug the original leak, and meanwhile more oil kept erupting. The slick eventually covered an 800-square-mile area.

The "invasion" of black substance hit Gaviota Beach, some of it in big chunks. Birds on the beach were coated with oil and unable to fly; scores of dead ones were washed ashore. It was difficult to calculate the damage to marine life, but some studies indicated that as many as 15,000 fowl died.

The 1969 oil spill awakened people and launched the nation's most intense environmental movement to date. Petitions were circulated to end offshore oil exploration; tougher regulations and new laws evolved. The spill influenced Congress to enact the Federal Water Pollution Control Act and to toughen standards in the Outer Continental Shelf Lands Act of 1970. It was also the impetus for the passage by voters of Proposition 20 in 1972, which established the California Coastal Commission.

Freedom Train. Gaviota saw Southern Pacific engine #4449, the steam locomotive that powered the Freedom Train, come across its trestle. This train was one of the most historic accomplishments of the nation's bicentennial celebration in 1975-1976. It was a privately-sponsored venture which took historical documents and artifacts around the country, traveling more than twenty-four thousand miles through the forty-eight contiguous states. Five hours were required to set up displays in the ten cars at each stop, and other railroad traffic could not be interrupted.

Locomotive #4449 was one of two that had to be rebuilt for the journey. It had formerly pulled passenger trains such as the *Daylight* and the *Lark* up and down the Gaviota coast in the early 1940s. After diesel engines came into use, it had been retired from service on October 2, 1957, to be put on permanent display in a city park in Portland, Oregon. More than 20,000 hours of work were required to rebuild the 425-ton engine.

After the Freedom Train completed its national run, the locomotive itself continued to pull special trains. In May and June 1984, it went from Portland to the World's Fair in New Orleans via the California coast route, and it again crossed the trestle at Gaviota on its return journey on

The Freedom Train steams over the Gaviota trestle.

June 19, 1984. Gaviota was a favorite spot for photography, and after traversing the trestle, the train let people off, then backed up and recrossed, blowing smoke. The same engine again came through Gaviota on May 4, 1989, going south to take part in the fiftieth anniversary of Union Station in Los Angeles. It also appeared with Kirk Douglas and Burt Lancaster in the 1986 movie *Tough Guys*. A picture of the train appeared in the July 1990 issue of *Trains* as it cruised across the "high bridge" at Gaviota.

Ancient Fossils. Part of the history that has been "written" in the cliffs at Gaviota became visible in January 1988, when a three-foot fossil was found east of the beach. It was thought to be ten million years old and considered the largest halibut skeleton of its age to be recovered in California—possibly in the entire United States. It required many hours of chipping and cutting before a 300-pound rock slab containing the petrified remains was freed. A team of five worked late into the afternoon but had to stop for darkness. There was concern that pounding surf and abnormally high night tides might cause damage, as the fossil was located on the rock surface. The operation was a success, however, and the skeleton was to be loaned to the museum in Los Angeles. The newspapers and television carried the story, and casts were to be made for distribution to various research groups.

Another fossil was located about three miles east of Gaviota Beach in

June 1992 by Stephen Moat, and Gaviota again was on television and in newspapers. The specimen was a marine mammal measuring two and one-half feet across and was thought to be an ancient seal rather than a fish or porpoise. The well-preserved skeleton was estimated to be eight million years old and would help to tell about life in the Gaviota Land then. It is thought that it died and sank about 1,000 feet to the sea bottom, which is now dry land. After several days of hard work, the 400-pound rock was lifted up the rugged cliffs to Highway 101, to be placed on a flatbed truck for transportation to Santa Barbara City College. At least four plaster castings would be distributed for study. The Gaviota Land had again yielded part of its ancient life to the people of the present.

Fossil fish found at Gaviota.

CHAPTER 15
Big Oil

Early Operations

Large oil deposits have been found in the ocean near Gaviota, and the results have greatly affected the Gaviota Land. One of the first oil findings on the ocean edge was down the beach from Gaviota at Summerland in March 1894. H.L. Williams, a spiritualist leader, had sold lots to his followers, and oil was found while digging for water on their parcels. Soon a forest of wooden derricks was built along the beach, and others later went out into the water on stilts. This was the first sea drilling in American history, and the rigs were the first submarine oil wells in tidelands. An estimated one hundred sixty-five wells were drilled by twenty-two oil companies, and the Seaside Oil Company (later Tidewater Oil Company) was established to refine the crude. The Summerland wells were not very deep, however, and most activity had ceased by 1920. Although the derricks were no longer visible, the wells on the ocean floor had not been properly plugged when they were abandoned, and they continued to leak oil. In 1992, the Coastal Commission approved $810,000 to cap three of them.

Another important oil strike was at Ellwood, also east of Gaviota, in 1927, and other piers were built into the surf there. The Rio Grande Oil Company and the Barnsdall Oil Company were in exploration partnership, and the test well "came in" just minutes before the project was to be abandoned. This was to be the first real oil producer off the coast, as the Summerland wells had been very shallow. Geological studies indicated, however, that the bulk of the oil was out under the sea.

219

The first American offshore oil wells at Summerland.

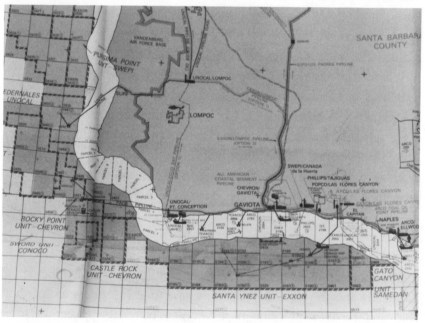

U.S. Department of the Interior map of offshore oil leases.

Platform Helen dismantled by a crane.

The State Lands Commission governs tidelands from mean high tide to three miles out, and the federal Minerals Management Service of the Department of the Interior controls the outer continental shelf, which extends out an additional 200 nautical miles. Oil discoveries in the ocean led to leases in both areas, and practically all major oil companies were conducting explorations in 1956 to obtain information for bidding on the right to develop. As fields were found, platforms began to emerge, and onshore industrial support facilities were erected to handle their production.

Platforms Harry, Herman, and Helen

Three platforms in state waters offshore from the Gaviota Land were part of channel life for years. From the west, they were Harry, Herman, and Helen, the latter only five miles from Gaviota. Harry, a twenty-four-well platform owned by Phillips Petroleum Company, began operations in about 1961, was abandoned in 1973, and taken down in 1974. Texaco and two partners paid $23.7 million for the leases of Helen and Herman. Helen, built in two sections, had twenty-eight wells and went into production in September 1960. Herman, a satellite facility gathering point for about ten undersea wellheads, was installed in 1964.

Helen was shut down in 1973, and Herman was closed in 1983. They were both removed from the ocean bottom in May 1988. Herman was eliminated in one section, but Helen had to be removed by a 400-ton crane in two segments, and a large barge transported the steel to Santa Monica Bay, where plans were to submerge it for an artificial reef. The platforms were missed by navigators of small boats, as they had often been used to triangulate and locate fishing reefs. Application was made in April 1992 for the abandonment and site restoration of the Texaco Gaviota Oil and Gas Processing Facility, located west of the marine terminal.

The Santa Ynez Unit

A new oil era opened up with the first big sale of federal leases off southern California in February 1968. One hundred ten tracts in deep waters were available, totaling about 500,000 acres. The Santa Ynez Unit was a glimpse of the big oil boom to come in the channel off Gaviota. Exxon bought forty-seven tracts, and twenty of these (more than 97,000 acres) became known as the Santa Ynez Unit. Chevron and Shell were also partners, but Exxon was the designated operator. Substantial quantities of oil and gas were discovered in three fields: Hondo, Pescado, and Sacate.

In these three domains, four platforms were to be erected from three to nine miles off Gaviota's shores: The first platform, Hondo (twenty-eight wells) was erected in June 1976 and began production in the Hondo field in April 1981. Platform Harmony (sixty wells) would further tap this field; Heritage (also sixty wells) would pump the Pescado field, and Heather (twenty-eight wells) was proposed to operate in the Secate field.

The metal "jacket" for Harmony was towed all the way from Korea to Gaviota, where it was sunk in federal waters slightly to the east of the beach on June 21, 1989, after it had been tugged back and forth for days while tariff and duty fees were resolved. The 1,480-foot platform was taller than the Empire State Building in New York. Most of its 44,000 tons, however, were under water; only about 280 feet would be visible. Harmony's "sister," Heritage, Exxon's second largest platform (1,100 feet tall and weighing 35,000 tons), was sunk on October 7, 1989. Depending on production levels, projections were to install Heather around 1994.

To process the oil and gas from the platforms, Exxon proposed to build a huge processing facility in Las Flores Canyon near the Pacific Offshore Pipeline Company (POPCO) gas plant, but negotiations collapsed over pollution controls. For several years, disagreements, bitter debates, and lawsuits followed between the company, the county, and the state. Exxon consequently went beyond the county's jurisdiction to process, store, and ship the oil from an offshore storage and treating vessel (OS&T), located in federal waters. A large ship was modified to remove the water and hydrogen sulfide from the oil before it went to refineries. After years of further hearings, debates, and negotiations, however, Exxon's massive $2.5-billion onshore facility was finally approved by the county, and ground was broken on April 8, 1988. Part of the agreement was the later removal of the offshore storage and treating vessel.

Celeron/All American Pipeline

The large quantities of oil and gas discovered required transportation to refineries, and two possible choices were the Celeron/All American pipeline to Texas and a permanent marine terminal at either Las Flores Canyon or Gaviota.

Celeron Pipeline Company, a subsidiary of the Goodyear Tire Corporation, began building an interstate pipeline in 1985. This was the nation's

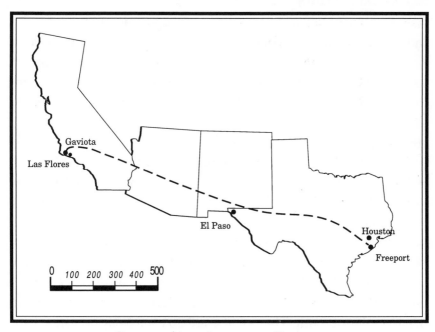

CELERON/ALL AMERICAN PIPELINE

first west coast to gulf coast oil pipeline, linking the oil off the coast of Gaviota (and some from the San Joaquin Valley) with refineries in Texas. It was longer than the well-known Alaskan pipeline and stretched from Gaviota across four states to reach its destination. A coastal segment also went from Gaviota to Las Flores Canyon. About 300,000 barrels of crude could be propelled 1,768 miles in 18 days. It would require 231 pumping and heating stations to keep the oil liquid, 3 of which would be located in Santa Barbara County. A $4-million computer system would monitor the 30-inch line for ruptures, flow rates, and temperatures. The $1 billion project was a massive undertaking, employing thousands of people.

The Celeron pipeline entered Santa Barbara County on May 10, 1986, and in the next three or four months, hundreds of miles of pipe were placed in the ground as it traversed hills and valleys for about seventy miles, slithering like a gigantic metal snake. Around 2,500 oak trees had to be removed. The Celeron Pipeline Company of California merged with the All American Pipeline Company on May 31, 1989.

Gaviota Marine Terminal

Tankering was an alternative method of transportation to the refineries, and a large, interim terminal for this purpose was constructed at Gaviota. Texaco purchased the Getty Trading and Transportation Company in about 1983, and the Texaco Trade and Transportation Company became the controlling partner in the new multi-million-dollar interim Gaviota Marine Terminal, a joint venture including Chevron, Exxon, Phillips, and other subsidiary companies.

The $50-million terminal would be permitted to ship 100,000 barrels of crude a day. Three new tanks on the 46-acre site would provide storage for more than half a million barrels, and a tanker mooring and loading facility would be installed 3,500 feet offshore with a new pipeline, which would load an estimated 156 tankers per year. In order to position the pipeline, a temporary pier had to be built 700 feet into the ocean. The pipeline was laid in a fifteen-foot trench of the thirty-two-foot-wide trestle and weighted with rocks. Approximately 220 truck loads came from Solvang in one month. The trestle was then completely dismantled and all the pilings removed.

Temporary pier built at Gaviota to construct new tanker-loading facility.

Gaviota Marine Terminal.

The Gaviota Marine Terminal was initially intended to be temporary, operating only until All American (Celeron) and other pipelines were operational. A consolidated marine terminal was under consideration at Exxon's immense facility in Las Flores Canyon, but Exxon requested that construction of its project be deferred, and Texaco filed with the county to establish the Gaviota Terminal as the permanent south coast facility. This would increase the permitted number of barrels per day to 125,000 and the frequency of tanker visits to 196 per year. Although the exportation of oil

225

to refineries was the primary consideration for the terminal, it could not be ruled out that Alaskan crude might go to Texas from the terminal, and this would mean the mooring of additional tankers off Gaviota and greatly augmented travel through the channel.

The Point Arguello Project and Gaviota Processing Facility

Chevron, U.S.A., Inc. and its partners won leases in the Point Arguello area of the Santa Barbara Channel in June 1979, and adjacent areas were acquired in May 1981. (After Lease Sale 80 on October 17, 1984, a moratorium put other sales on hold.) Enormous oil discoveries were made in these leases off Point Conception in the Santa Maria Basin. It was considered the largest "find" to date in federal waters and a massive domestic strike. It was thought to be one of the biggest Chevron projects in the world, and it changed the Gaviota Land.

Three metal jackets for three platforms, Harvest (Texaco), Hidalgo (Chevron) and Hermosa (Chevron), were installed ten to fifteen miles offshore in 1985-86. Hermosa was designed to operate forty-eight wells, Hidalgo fifty-six, and Harvest fifty. Platform Hidalgo, for example, could accommodate more than ninety people in its living quarters, and employees worked every other seven days in twelve-hour shifts. Transportation to the platform was usually by air from the Santa Maria airport.

A processing facility to handle this immense find was erected at Gaviota. It had the capacity to accommodate up to 250,000 barrels of oil and 110 million cubic feet of natural gas per day. Pipelines transporting crude from the platforms to the processing center extended under ten miles of ocean and eighteen of land. A twenty-four-inch oil pipeline and a twenty-inch gas pipeline sent raw oil and gas from Harvest and Hidalgo to Hermosa, whence all went to landfall at Point Conception. The pipelines continued across the Cojo and Hollister ranches, through Gaviota State Park, and under Highway 101 to reach the processing complex, which occupied about half of a sixty-five-acre site. Separate gas and oil plants were located on tiers, and Chevron was the operator for both. Water and hydrogen sulfide gas were separated from the crude, and the "dry oil" was sent to the Gaviota Marine Terminal to go to the refineries by either tanker or pipeline. Natural gas went to the Southern California Gas

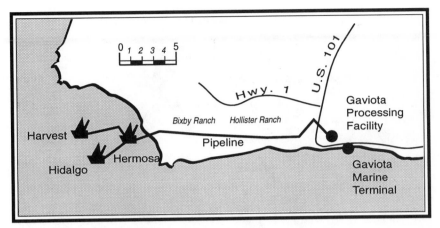

POINT ARGUELLO PROJECT

Company, and propane and butane were trucked from the site. A seawater desalination plant, which converted every thousand gallons of salt water into 300 gallons of fresh water, was part of the complex.

To consolidate the massive project, three partnerships were formed from eighteen companies. The Point Arguello Pipeline Company (PAPCO) handled the "wet" oil from Platform Hermosa to the oil treating plant and the line to the marine terminal. The Point Arguello Natural Gas Line Company (PANGLCO) owned the gas line from Platform Hermosa to Gaviota, and the Gaviota Gas Plant Company (GGP) controlled gas operations. Chevron was the managing partner for the complex.

Site preparation started during rain in November 1985, and heavy grading and other work were rapidly underway. The work continued almost around the clock, as hundreds of workers swarmed the hillsides of the Gaviota Land to quickly erect the processing center. The gulls squalled over the rumbling trucks below them. Pipelines stretched under the land for miles, like the tentacles of an octopus, and the complex soon sprawled over one of the most beautiful sections of the coast. The facility also included a freeway overpass, and on-ramps and off-ramps at Mariposa Reina. Extensive landscaping was to be done, as many trees and shrubs had to be replaced. The structures were to be screened from view of Highway 101 within five years. (This did not happen.) Other conditions required the

The Point Arguello pipeline as it passes through Gaviota State Park.

The Chevron refinery in an early stage of construction.

repaving of Hollister Ranch Road, $50,000 for ranch firefighting equipment, a permanent Vista Del Mar School, and a new fire station.

Gaviota Fire Station (#18). A fire station was considered necessary at Gaviota; the closest units, at Buellton and Goleta, were almost half an hour away, and numerous fires were possible from the large amounts of gas and oil being produced at Gaviota. The facility would also be an asset for numerous traffic accidents, and the state park, too, frequently required assistance. A temporary station to provide full-time protection was erected on the old Vista Del Mar School ground; it consisted of a modular trailer and one fire engine. The permanent fire station was built on the hill west

Gaviota Fire Station No. 18.

of the processing plant. The cost of the station was estimated to be almost $3 million, and negotiations could be opened in the future for the use of county funds.

During construction of the new station in April 1986, a full-scale alert caused the closure of Highway 101. An eight-inch pressure line had been ripped open by a bulldozer, and firefighters feared that a spark would ignite the leaking fuel. Hundreds of cars had to be detoured through San

Temporary Vista del Mar School site.

Marcos Pass; trains were stopped, and the Vista Del Mar School was evacuated.

Vista Del Mar School. The small one-school district did not want to leave its permanent home by the sea, but competition from "big oil" forced it to move to a temporary complex on an eighty-six-acre Chevron site about one and one-half miles east of its former location. The new school was erected in about three months in order to allow plant construction to begin right away. Flatbed trucks brought modular building components from Patterson, California, and a crew of up to one hundred people worked seventy hours a week to grade the land and erect the structures.

Part of the 3,400-square-foot classroom complex for kindergarten through eighth grade was a 25-station science room with computer terminals. There was also a soccer field with a running track around the perimeter. The caretaker's residence was a mobile trailer. The new school opened for approximately sixty students in February 1986, and ownership of the former site was claimed by others under reversionary clauses since it was no longer a school site.

Fifteen different sites for a permanent location were considered by the

230

school district. A section of the Orella Ranch was one of the finalists, but the first choice was the former site of the old Las Cruces School, although the sea view would be history. This property now belonged to the state, however, and although the area didn't have numerous visitors, the state didn't want to part with any of its land. There was concern about conversion of a park area for non-park uses. Negotiations between the school district, Chevron, and the Department of Parks and Recreation continued for several years.

During these negotiations, Chevron offered Gaviota State Park the buildings and improvements of the temporary school and ten acres of surrounding land in exchange for the Las Cruces site, two acres for the fire station, and pipeline rights through park property. It was felt that this would give the department additional acreage, new administrative facilities, and would release additional beach frontage for public use. The offer was refused.

The state also rejected school district offers for the park site, and the district initiated condemnation proceedings to acquire the land, but they were not successful. The school district had set aside $225,000 for the purchase, but after a two-week court trial, the judge ruled that the proposed school would not be compatible with the park, nor would it be a more necessary use of the land.

The school district then made another offer of $1.5 million, partly funded by Chevron, which was around seven times the actual value of the land, and politics and money reversed previous decisions. The state decided to reconsider the sale, and the bill AB 1246 was passed in Sacramento. It authorized the transfer of 16.7 acres of Gaviota State Park property to the Vista Del Mar School District as a special case, and the sale was finalized in October 1989.

It was hoped that this money would be put into improvements in the Gaviota Land, which had "paid the price." In the fall of 1990, however, $1.26 million from the sale of the park land to the school district was appropriated for the purchase of about 960 acres of chaparral adjacent to the La Purísima Mission in Lompoc. It was reported that the state also received about $3 million from Chevron for the pipeline sepulchers in the Gaviota Land.

Vista de Las Cruces School.

Just before the Vista Del Mar School moved to its temporary facility, it was found out that classrooms had been near soil contaminated with cancer-causing, toxic polychlorinated biphenyls (PCBs) on the Chevron construction site. Chevron had negotiated with Getty in the 1960s to build a gas processing plant on a seven-acre parcel north of the highway from Getty's terminal (a second gas plant was also later installed), and incomplete flushing when the plant was dismantled in 1984 caused the contamination. There was a communication failure, however, and the county wasn't notified until months later. Workers wearing protective clothing loaded the soil on trucks, and it was taken to the hazardous waste dump in Kettleman City, Kern County.

After more than six years, a large, beautiful new $17-million school complex opened for over one hundred students in Las Cruces in the fall of 1992. The new school also had a new name: Vista de Las Cruces. The temporary school building was to be dismantled and donated to the Santa Ynez Valley Christian Academy in Solvang.

Hazards and Risks. Although Chevron's immense processing facility was permitted by the county in December 1984, most people were not aware of the extent of the project, but some did try to contest the decision. Vista Del Mar School District had endeavored to keep its home, but lost it anyway. The Hollister and Cojo residents also battled to preserve the safety

Chevron refinery at Mariposa Reina.

and seclusion of their land, but they, too, failed. The state initially objected to the pipelines in its recreational sanctuary, but was no longer vocal after around $4.5 million in compensation trickled into the treasury.

A Ventura County judge, through eminent domain, granted Chevron and partners the legal right to install the controversial pipelines in 100-foot rights of way through the Cojo region, through approximately thirty oceanfront parcels on Hollister Ranch, and across Gaviota State Beach. Chevron made financial settlements to some of the residents for the loss in value of their land. Some angry land owners tried to delay the work. One person blocked access to construction crews with his truck and tractor, but a tow vehicle removed them.

The processing complex itself went in not far from heavily populated rest areas, a state park used daily by hundreds of people, and next to a major highway traveled by thousands. There was danger from ruptures, leaks, explosions, and fires. The pipelines entombed in the ground carried hydrogen sulfide, a deadly and lethal gas found mixed with underground oil reserves and known to be one of the most toxic of chemicals. At low concentrations, hydrogen sulfide has an obnoxious odor similar to that of rotten eggs, but at higher levels, the colorless gas is odorless and can quickly be lethal. Both the central nervous and respiratory systems are affected, and coma and lung paralysis can occur in a very short time.

The county permit to transport oil and gas in pipelines onshore was initially based on hydrogen sulfide concentrations of 7,000 parts per million (ppm), which was dangerous, but Hollister attorneys found out that

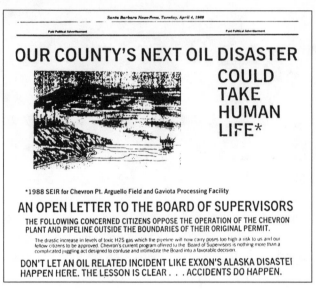

Santa Barbara News-Press, Tuesday, April 4, 1989

Paid Political Advertisement   Paid Political Advertisement

OUR COUNTY'S NEXT OIL DISASTER COULD TAKE HUMAN LIFE*

*1988 SEIR for Chevron Pt. Arguello Field and Gaviota Processing Facility

AN OPEN LETTER TO THE BOARD OF SUPERVISORS

THE FOLLOWING CONCERNED CITIZENS OPPOSE THE OPERATION OF THE CHEVRON PLANT AND PIPELINE OUTSIDE THE BOUNDARIES OF THEIR ORIGINAL PERMIT.

The drastic increase in levels of toxic H2S gas which the pipeline will now carry poses too high a risk to us and our fellow citizens to be approved. Chevron's current program offered to the Board of Supervisors is nothing more than a complicated juggling act designed to confuse and intimidate the Board into a favorable decision.

DON'T LET AN OIL RELATED INCIDENT LIKE EXXON'S ALASKA DISASTEI HAPPEN HERE. THE LESSON IS CLEAR . . . ACCIDENTS DO HAPPEN.

The controversy over oil development in the Gaviota Land.

the actual "sour gas" content might be as high as 20,000 ppm. At this news, many people felt that this was the second time (following the contaminated soil incident) in two years that there had been silence on reporting potential dangers and threats to the public.

Public and government awareness of the increased concentrations of hydrogen sulfide resulted in many public hearings, first by the Santa Barbara County Planning Commission and then by the Board of Supervisors. Most of these meetings were standing-room-only affairs, and thousands of other citizens watched on television. It was determined that a Supplemental Environmental Impact Review was necessary to determine whether Chevron's operation was now in "substantial conformity" with the original permit. Toxic flammable vapor clouds, hazard zone "footprints," winds, heights, and distances were calculated and recalculated in different scenarios. Newspapers contained many articles and full-page ads supporting both sides as the controversy raged on over the decisions involved in the Gaviota Land. Lawyers and specialists were called in, and many individuals spoke against the higher levels of sour gas. A threat by the state to close Gaviota State Beach again prompted calls to return it to the county.

On December 20, 1988, the Planning Commission voted unanimously against certifying the project at the higher hydrogen sulfide level, but Chevron appealed that decision to the Board of Supervisors to seek an overruling. Other hotly debated public hearings were held and televised. On April 4, 1989, however, the Board of Supervisors went over the Planning Commission and reversed their refusal. Chevron was found to be in substantial conformity, and the project was given approval. The risks were deemed "acceptable."

A leak detection system was provided for Hollister Ranch. Two bulletin boards were installed at Gaviota Beach in April 1989 to provide written forewarning of possible dangers, but most of the information posted there was environmental. Two loudspeakers were placed on the quiet hillside in July 1989 for audible warnings. There was only one narrow exit road out of the beach area, however, and that was shared with all of the Hollister residents. Quick access to busy Highway 101 was very difficult at best, and a panic or an accident could cause a complete blockade.

Many people felt that if the county had been aware of the situation in the beginning, different arrangements would have been made for the Chevron project. The vote for the onshore route by the Planning Commission in 1984 had been split three to two. Alternatives would have been to remove the hydrogen sulfide at sea or to inject it back into the ground. Both of these methods had been used elsewhere. A processing facility at landfall (Point Conception), would have removed much of the danger from the populated areas.

Chevron was at last permitted to start up, but it did not do so because the company wanted to use tankers for transportation to refineries instead of the pipelines which had been agreed to in the permit process. The

Bullhorns are part of the new Gaviota warning system.

county preferred pipelines in order to avoid an ocean oil spill. The big channel disaster in 1969 and the estimated eleven-million-gallon *Exxon Valdez* oil spill in Alaska in March 1989 still floated in local memories. To allow time for pipeline arrangements to be made, however, the county granted a temporary tanker permit in May 1989, but this was overturned by the California Coastal Commission.

The oil situation at Gaviota even received considerable concern from the federal government. Production and reserves became world headlines after Iraq invaded Kuwait in the summer of 1990, and the controversy over oil at Gaviota drew national attention.

Chevron initiated the process for an enduring tanker permit, but the request was denied by the Board of Supervisors on November 12, 1990. It was felt that tankering would pose a much greater environmental threat, and that the original permit agreement was not being adhered to. Chevron appealed the denial decision to the California Coastal Commission, but on April 10, 1991, the appeal was denied.

There were existing pipelines which could carry Chevron's crude. One went to Kern County, then to Los Angeles (All American Pipeline and Four Corners Pipeline Company's Line 63); another All American pipeline was available to Texas. Oil could also be piped to the San Francisco area, and under consideration was the construction of a Chevron-built pipeline to Los Angeles using the right of way of the Southern Pacific railroad.

Using the existing pipelines, Chevron decided at last to begin pumping oil in May 1991, and the oil reached the processing center around June 15 of that year. Television cameras were on hand to film the first few drops arriving from the massive domestic oil field. They were displayed in a glass jar, and the Point Arguello project was at last operational.

It was thought that things would go smoothly now. Wrong! The oil industry still strived for that crude "foot" in the tanker "door." Chevron instigated a $100-million lawsuit against the county and went to the state level to seek a tanker permit from the California Coastal Commission, bypassing county authority. Eight confidential discussions were held before another four-hour, standing-room-only hearing in Santa Barbara on April 6, 1992. Many citizens were upset and concerned, calling the scheme a sellout to the oil industry, and the Coastal Commission shelved the plan. Chevron then appealed to the county again for a three-year tankering permit, indicating they would sign a pipeline contract after fifteen months of market "testing." After long hours of hearings, the county voted to allow Chevron twenty months of tankering to Los Angeles, but only after a binding contract had been signed with a pipeline company. Chevron contested this and applied again to the Coastal Commission to override the county's decision, and the commission allowed Chevron to begin tankering right away after 40,000 barrels per day had been sent by pipeline. Chevron was to cease sending Point Arguello crude to the Bay Area by pipeline in order to tanker it to Los Angeles. A pipeline construction contract is to be signed by February 1, 1994, and the pipeline must be completed by January 1, 1996, after which all tankering from Gaviota will cease; but this decision is being appealed.

Sunset over the Gaviota Land.

Epilogue

The Gaviota Land lies close to the bend of the continent where the coastline changes and the ocean becomes a different sea. It is an abrupt turn on El Camino Real, where traveling civilization turns sharply to change directions. People today still follow the same route as those in past history. Travelers going south instantaneously experience a beautiful panorama of the Pacific Ocean at the sudden turn at the top of the hill at Gaviota. To the migrating population going north, Gaviota is the coastal gateway to northern California as the road leads through the unique Gaviota Pass.

This has been the land of the Chumash. It was part of one of the first land grants in the county. It has experienced immense earthquakes, a simoon, heavy rains, and drought. The expeditions of Portolá and De Anza passed through Gaviota. Hides and tallow were traded off its shores, and the land's remoteness made it a natural site for smuggling. Stagecoaches rolled over the land, and bandits were also part of the colorful past. The old wharf was a hub of commerce and shipping for large ocean-going vessels. Long, hot cattle drives were made to the wharf and later to the railroad when the last of the "Gap" was closed there. The land is now part of the state of California, and "big oil" has had great influence on the area. The story of the Gaviota Land has been a small part of California history; but it is also unique in having its own special past.

Bibliography

Books

All Aboard America. The American Freedom Train Foundation, Inc., 1976.

Anza's California Expeditions, vol. IV: Font's Complete Diary of the Second Anza Expedition. Translated and edited by Herbert Bolton. Berkeley: University of California Press, 1930.

Bancroft, Herbert Howe. *The Works of Hubert Howe Bancroft, History of California*. Santa Barbara: Wallace Hebberd, 1963.

Bell, Katherine M. *Swinging The Censer, Reminiscences of Old Santa Barbara*. Hartford: Finlay Press, 1931.

Benefield, Hattie Stone. *For The Good Of The Country*. Los Angeles: Lorrin Morrison, 1951.

Best, Gerald M. *Ships and Narrow Gauge Rails*. Berkeley: Howell-North, 1964.

Bolton, Herbert Eugene. *An Outpost of Empire*. New York: Russell and Russell, 1965.

Brewer, William H. *Up and Down California in 1860-1864, The Journal of William H. Brewer*. Berkeley: University of California Press, 1966.

Chase, J. Smeaton. *California Coast Trails, A Horseback Ride from Mexico to Oregon*. Boston and New York: Houghton Mifflin Company, 1913.

Chesnut, Merlyn. *Gaviota Pass and Gaviota Beach, A History*. Unpublished. California State University, San Luis Obispo, 1969.

Cleland, Robert Glass. *From Wilderness to Empire, A History of California 1542-1900*. New York: Alfred A. Knopf, 1944.

Cowan, Robert. *Ranchos of California*. Los Angeles: Historical Society of Southern California, 1977.

Dana, Richard Henry, Jr. *Two Years Before The Mast*. Cornwall: Dodd, Mead and Company, 1946.

Davis, William Heath. *Seventy-Five Years in California*. San Francisco: John Howell Books, 1967.

Davison, Grace L. *The Gates of Memory*. Solvang: Santa Ynez Valley *News*, 1955.

Dibblee, R.W., Jr. *Geology of Southwestern Santa Barbara County, California*. Bulletin 150. San Francisco: Division of Mines, 1950.

Englehardt, R. Zephryin, O.F.M. *Santa Barbara, Queen of the Missions*. San Francisco: The James H. Barry Company, 1923.

Grant, Campbell. *The Rock Paintings of the Chumash*. Berkeley: University of California Press, 1965.

Hawley, Walter A. *The Early Days of Santa Barbara, California*. Santa Barbara: Schauer Printing Studio, 1920.

Heath, E. M. *Guide and Map of Santa Barbara and Surrounding Country*. Revised by W. W. Osborne. Santa Barbara: W.W. Osborne, 1940.

Heizer, R. F. and M.A. Whipple, editors. *The California Indians, A Source Book*. Berkeley: University of California Press, 1960.

Hittell, Theodore H. *History of California*. Vol. II. San Francisco: J.J. Stone & Company, 1897.

Kallman, Robert E. and Eugene Wheeler. *Coastal Crude In A Sea of Conflict*. San Luis Obispo: Blake Printery & Pub. Co., 1984.

Kroeber, A. L. *Handbook of the Indians of California*. Berkeley: California Book Company, Ltd., 1953.

Librado, Fernando. *The Eye of the Flute, Chumash Traditional History and Ritual as Told by Fernando Librado Kitsepawit to John P. Harrington*. Banning, California: The Malki Museum Press, 1977.

Mason, Jesse. *A History of Santa Barbara and Ventura Counties*. Oakland: Thompson and West, 1883.

McGowan, Edward. *California Vigilantes*. Oakland: Biobooks, 1946.

Marinacci, Barbara and Rudy. *California's Spanish Place-Names*. San Rafael, California: Presidio Press, 1980.

Mink, James. *The Santa Ynez Valley*. Unpublished. University of California, Los Angeles, 1949.

Nostrand, Richard Lee. *A Settlement Geography of the Santa Ynez Valley, California*. Unpublished. University of California, Los Angeles, 1964.

O'Neill, Owen H. *History of Santa Barbara County, Its People and Its Resources*. Santa Barbara: Harold McLean Meier, 1939.

Ord, Angustias de la Guerra. *Occurrences in Hispanic California*. Translated and edited by Francis Price and William H. Ellison. Richmond: The William Byrd Press, Inc., 1956.

Orr, Phil C. *Prehistory of Santa Rosa Island*. Santa Barbara: Santa Barbara Museum of Natural History, 1968.

Outland, Charles F. *Stagecoaching on the El Camino Real, Los Angeles to San Francisco, 1861-1901*. Glendale, California: The Arthur H. Clark Company, 1973.

Palou, Fray Francisco, O.F.M. *Historical Memoirs of New California*. Vol. II. Translated into English from the manuscript in the Archives of Mexico. Edited by Herbert Eugene Bolton. Berkeley: University of California Press, 1926.

Paulson, L.L. *Hand-Book and Directory of San Luis Obispo, Santa Barbara, Ventura, Kern, San Bernardino, Los Angeles & San Diego*. San Francisco, 1875.

Phillips, Michael James. *Santa Barbara County, California*. Vol. I. Los Angeles: The S.J. Clark Publishing Company, 1927.

Poett, A. Dibblee. *Rancho San Julian, the Story of a California Ranch and Its People*. Santa Barbara: Fithian Press/Santa Barbara Historical Society, 1991.

Rife, Joanne. *Where the Light Turns Gold, The Story of the Santa Ynez Valley*. Fresno: Valley Publishers, 1977.

Rogers, David Banks. *Prehistoric Man of the Santa Barbara Coast*. Santa Barbara: Santa Barbara Museum of Natural History, 1929.

Ruth, Clarence. *A Survey of Fifty Pre-Historic Chumash Indian Village Sites, 1930-1967*. Unpublished. Lompoc, 1967.

Storke, Yda Addis. *A Memorial and Biographical History of the Counties of Santa Barbara, San Luis Obispo, and Ventura, California*. Chicago: The Lewis Publishing Company, 1891.

The Portolá Expedition of 1769-1770. Diary of Miguel Costans. Edited by Frederick J. Teggard. Berkeley: Academy of Pacific Coast History, 1911.

Tompkins, Walker A. *Goleta, The Good Land*. Goleta: Goleta Amvets Post No. 55 and Santa Barbara *News-Press*, 1966.

——*Old Spanish Santa Barbara*. Illustrated by Russell Ruiz. Santa Barbara: McNally and Loftin, 1967.

——*Santa Barbara's Royal Rancho*. Berkeley: Nowell-North, 1961.

——*Stagecoach Days in Santa Barbara County*. Santa Barbara: McNally & Loftin, 1982.

——*Yankie Barbareños*. Unpublished. Santa Barbara.

Wheeler, Eugene and Robert Kallman. *Shipwrecks, Smugglers and Maritime Mysteries*. Ventura, California: Pathfinder Publishing, 1986.

Pamphlets, Reports, and Periodicals

Anderson, Jr., Eugene. *The Chumash Indians of Southern California*. Banning, California: Malki Museum Press, 1968.

Applegate, Dr. Richard. *An Index of Chumash Placenames*. San Luis Obispo County Archaeological Society Occasional Papers No. 9, 1975.

Baxter, Don J. *Gateways to California, Gaviota and San Marcos Passes*. San Francisco: Pacific Gas and Electric Company, 1968.

California Highways and Public Works Magazine. Multiple dates.

Chevron U.S.A., Inc. *Point Arguello Platforms*. Ventura, California.

Cultural Resources Report, Gaviota Interim Marine Termial. Texaco Trading and Transportation, Inc. Santa Barbara: Westec Services, Inc., 1988.

Cultural Resources Report for the All American Pipeline Project. All American Pipeline Co., New Mexico State University, 1989.

Environmental Impact Report for the Proposed Vista Del Mar School at Las Cruces, Land Acquisition and Property Development. Santa Barbara: The Planning Corporation of Santa Barbara, 1987.

Gaviota State Beach Expansion Study, Supplemental Report. State of California Division of Beaches and Parks, 1967.

In the Beautiful Santa Ynez Valley and *Adventure in the Santa Ynez Valley*. Santa Ynez Valley News. Santa Ynez: Multiple dates.

King, Chester. *The Names and Locations of Historic Chumash Villages*. Journal of California Anthropology, Vol. 2, No. 2.

Lawler, Nan. *Closing the Gap*. (Reprinted from *Railroad History Bulletin* No. 145, Autumn 1981). Goleta, California: Kimberly Press, 1984.

Lompoc Legacy. Quarterly Bulletin, Lompoc Valley Historical Society. Lompoc: Multiple dates.

Noticias. Quarterly Bulletin, Santa Barbara Historical Society. Santa Barbara: Multiple dates.

Santa Barbara County. *Chevron Point Arguello Field and Gaviota Processing Facility, Supplemental EIR*. Santa Barbara: Arthur D. Little, Inc., 1988.

Santa Barbara Museum of Natural History. *California's Chumash Indians*. Santa Barbara: John Daniel, Publisher, 1986.

Santa Barbara/Ventura Coastal State Park System General Plan. Sacramento: Department of Parks & Recreation, 1979.

The Point Arguello Companies. *Gaviota Plant and Pipelines*. Gaviota, California.

U.S. Department of Commerce, Coast and Geodetic Survey. *Tsunami*. Washington, D.C.: U.S. Government Printing Office.

U.S. Department of the Interior, Minerals Management Service. *Pacific Update: August 1987-November 1989, Outer Continental Shelf Oil & Gas Activities.* Hemdon, Virginia 1990.

Zarakov, Barry. *The Las Cruces Adobe and Its Relationship to the Central Coast Adobe Tradition.* Unpublished.

——*A History of the Las Cruces Adobe.* Unpublished. 1975.

Newspapers

Lompoc *Record* (multiple issues)

Santa Ynez *Valley News* (multiple issues)

Santa Barbara *News-Press* (multiple issues)

INTERVIEWS

Armas, Jinny, July 7, 1989.

Avila, Arnold, May 1, 1990.

Begg, John, November 23, 1968.

Begg, LeRoy, June 17 and 27, 1988.

Blakley, Jim, April 18, 1987.

Bobbit, Roy, August 2, 1990.

Bonilla, Isaac (Ike) A., May 1, 1990.

Carpenter, Robert, July 9, 1988.

Centeno, Juanita, June 3 and 16, l989.

Clancy, Tom, May 23, 1988.

Cordero, Frank, January 16, 1989.

Cota, Grace, April 19, 1990.

Creps, Mel and Ruth, May 21, 1988.

Day, Harry, March 28, 1990.

Dutra, Rose, June 27, 1988.

Fitzgerald, Dennis, November 30, 1989.

Fitzgerald, Rena, December 7, 1989.

Fletcher, Margaret (Peggy), May 28, 1988.

Foode, Charlie, May 21, 22, 23, and 26, 1988.

Fraters, Estelle, November 13, 1989.

Hall, Mrs. W., November 18 and 23, 1968.

Hapgood, Arthur, October 4, 1968.

Hansen, Don, September 15, 1988.

Henning, Caroline, November 27, 1989; April 18, and 29, 1990.

Henning, Walter, March 25, 1990; April 9, 1990.

Limes, Dean Lawrence, June 23, 1988.

Limes, June, May 26, 1988.

Loustalot, Cesarina, November 3, 1968; December 1, 1988.

Loustalot, Jean, March 22, 1990.

Luis, Joe and Helen, June 8, 1989.

Lunsford, Mike, June 11, 1992.

Lyons, Jeanette, November 3, 1968.

McDonell, John S., October 12, 1968, June 10, 1969.

Mickey, Russell, May 23, 1988.

Poett, A. Dibblee, April 5, 1989; October 18, 1989; March 12, 1990.

Rivaldi, Attilo, January 12 and 16, 1989.

Ruiz, Russell, October 12, 1968.

Ruth, Clarence, October 12, 1968.

Saralegui, Bernard, April 17, 1987.

Stone, Dale, September 15, 1988.

Tautrim, Luzina, November 15, 1989.

Thygesen, Hank, July 5, 1988.

Tompkins, Walker, October 19, 1968.

Tucker, Donna, March 12 and 27, 1989.

Wilson, Raymond (Dutch), March 12 and 20, 1990.

INDEX

248

Please send me
The Gaviota Land

____ copies @ $14.95 each (paperback)   = _____
California sales tax ($1.16 per copy, CA only)   + _____
Shipping (per order)   + $2.00
TOTAL   = $ _____

Name _____

Address _____

City/State/Zip _____

Return with check or money order to:
Merlyn Chesnut
332 Amherst Place
Lompoc, CA 93436
☐ *Check for autographed copy.*

Or order from:
Fithian Press
Post Office Box 1525
Santa Barbara, CA 93102

Check, money order, Visa and Master Card accepted.
☐ My check is enclosed.
☐ Please bill my Mastercard/Visa.
     Number_____ Expires_____

Or order by phone toll-free: (800) 662-8351